THE DREAM ENABLER

REFERENCE GUIDE

MATTHEW BURGESS

National Library of Australia Cataloguing-in-Publication entry

Creator: Burgess, Matthew, author.

Title: The Dream Enabler—Reference Guide/ Matthew Burgess; book designed by Dedicated Book Services.

ISBN: 978-1-925406-22-1 (paperback)

ISBN: 978-1-925406-23-8 (ebook : Kindle)

ISBN: 978-1-925406-24-5 (ebook : epub)

Subjects: Burgess, Matthew.
Law—Australia—Anecdotes
Practice of law—Australia—Anecdotes.
Lawyers—Australia—Anecdotes.

Other Creators/Contributors: Dedicated Book Services, book designer.

Dewey Number: 349.94

The Dream Enabler—Reference Guide

Published by D & M Fancy Pastry in 2016

Typefaces: ElectraLTStd

Table of Contents

Foreword . . . . *v*

Section 1

101 TIPS FOR STAYING YOUNG AND FOOLISH **1**

Section 2

SOME FURTHER CONTEXT **25**

Know Your Phone 27

The Toothpaste Box Story 29

The Leg of Ham Story 30

The View Business Plan 31

Everything From The 1991 Radio Shack Ad I Now Do on My Iphone 34

Section 3

QUOTES TO NOTE **37**

Section 4

FURTHER READING..........................**77**

Bibliography 79

About the Author 94

Acknowledgement 96

Foreword

SINCE THE EARLY 2000s, I have had the opportunity to work for many incredibly successful and inspirational people, including a significant percentage of the members of the various 'Rich Lists'. My roles have varied widely however, ultimately, they have always involved helping people achieve a goal or vision that is part of their life's work.

Like most lawyers, I have had others attach labels to me over the years, including:

a the baby-faced assassin

b the lawyer to get when you don't want to deal with a lawyer

c the 'www' (why the wealthy win) guy.

Undoubtedly there have been many other labels that, even if I knew of them, they would probably not be printable.

Someone, who never appeared on any list, coined the one that has meant the most to me.

She was a small business operator and we helped to ensure she had a structure that allowed her to survive and ultimately prosper during a difficult start-up phase. Her label for what I do is 'The dream enabler' and that is the theme and title of one of my books.

As set out in the foreword to 'The Dream Enabler', for as long as I can remember, the obsessive study of great thinkers has been my favourite pastime.

One aspect of this has been my evolving approach to 'common placing'–that is, the constant collection and ordering of the ideas of others.

Common placing has evolved, for me, from simply hoarding as many of my favourite books as possible, to cataloguing separately my favourite extracts, re-cataloguing extracts into disciplines and themes and to summarising the extracts into a centralised, personal 'bible' loosely titled 'brain food'.

Undoubtedly, everyone has their own learning style.

Successful entrepreneurs generally embrace one or more of the following concepts:

(1) You can only join the dots with hindsight.
(2) Actively creating serendipity is important.
(3) Fail fast.
(4) Deliver a 'MVP' – i.e. a minimum viable product, and then iterate and iterate again.
(5) Embrace 'loose-tight' thinking.

This Reference Guide sets out much of the content that for me leverages each of the above concepts and in turn inspired me to write The Dream Enabler.

Most aspects, I hope, are self-explanatory.

The '101 tips for staying young and foolish' section is a play on a famous Steve Jobs quote 'stay hungry; stay foolish'. The creation of the table of 101 tips is largely as a result of my disciplined common placing over many years.

In particular, each of the businesses I have founded has been heavily influenced by an array of thinkers. The capturing of the key messages of those thinkers that have been most relevant for our various business interests saw the creation of many principles, stories and tips over an extended period of time.

While constantly evolving, the version of the table that appears here is the one that was used in founding View Legal in 2014.

The reason for using the word 'young' instead of 'hungry' is that it better captures the interpretation of the quote that resonates most with me; that is 'stay young' = maintain high levels of energy and enthusiasm; 'stay foolish' = ensure a beginners mindset is maintained as much as possible.

All of the material in this Reference Guide ultimately then evolved, with thanks again to common placing, into the following nine key attributes explored in The Dream Enabler, namely:

The three 'P's

(1)   passion

(2)   persistence

(3)   purpose

The three 'I's

(4)   incubate

(5)   inspire

(6)   invest

The three 'L's

(7) law

(8) learning

(9) leverage.

In addition to The Dream Enabler book, the material in this Reference Guide has helped create The Dream Enabler Workbook.

The Workbook is designed to provide a catalyst, or starting point, for your personal journey in each of the 9 attributes explored in The Dream Enabler.

While it is a companion to the book, there is certainly no reason that you need have read The Dream Enabler before exploring this Reference Guide or the Workbook.

This said, in areas where you are wanting to deepen your understanding about particular concepts, the comparative chapter in The Dream Enabler will provide the foundation for further learning.

A free electronic copy of this Reference Guide is available from –

www.thedreamenabler.com.au/referenceguide

My hope for this Reference Guide, the Workbook and ultimately The Dream Enabler is that it facilitates your personally focused common placing and that in turn provides the foundation for your continued learning and realising of your dreams.

Section 1

101 Tips for Staying Young and Foolish

No.	Concept	Explanation	Story/source
1	The preferred due date on time turnarounds if not today, is yesterday	Habitually, anyone we service will want things returned as fast as possible, and totally correct.	The best form of marketing you can ever do is the job that is in front of you – a vast amount of our business is built off the back of this one concept.
2	Rocks first time; every time	Every day should start with completion of your hardest, biggest and most important task – all other relevant tasks will magically still get done, so long as this approach is taken.	This is one of the key principles out of Stephen Covey's '7 Habits of Highly Effective People'. On YouTube, there are videos where he demonstrates the rock analogy using a fish tank. Twain also famously said that 'if the first thing you do in the morning is eat a live frog, you can go through the rest of the day knowing the worst is behind you'. Your frog is your worst, hardest or most critical (not urgent!) task, and you should do it first thing in the morning before ANYTHING else. Also see Brian Tracy's book of the same name.
3	Measure twice, cut once	In all of our work, preparation is twice as important as doing.	Anyone that has spent any time at all in manual labour tasks from sewing to carpentry knows that this concept must be a mantra.
4	Allow equal time for delivery of first cut to final delivery	If a task is being promised to a customer within 10 days, the first completed draft should be provided to the reviewer within the first 5 days. It will always take time for the various iterations following this first review, and as a courtesy, the amount of time allowed for that should be equal to the amount of time that was taken to produce the first cut.	This rule of thumb is critical to consider in the context of Parkinson's Law (as explained below).

No.	Concept	Explanation	Story/source
5	Parkinson's Law	This concept is one that has been proven countless times across many industries, particularly in the professional services firms that use time billing. The basic theme is that every task will expand to the maximum available duration. This causes significant risks and stress that should be avoided at all costs, and is part of the reason why the rock concept is so critical.	See the book written by C Northcote Parkinson of the same name.
6	Price is what you pay…	…and value is what you get. This is one of Warren Buffett's most famous quotes. In combination with a number of other themes in this table it explains why we only assist customers on a pre-agreed scope of work with upfront guaranteed fixed pricing.	While a long read, there is significant value in 'The Snowball: Warren Buffett and the Business of Life' (the biography about Warren Buffett by Alice Schroeder).
7	Murphy's Law	Everything that can go wrong will go wrong.	The entire legal industry is essentially founded on the concept of Murphy's Law.
8	Baker's Law	Ron Baker is a mentor for many businesses – he has written numerous books on pricing and also developed what he calls Baker's Law. Essentially, this means that bad customers drive out good customers because the heavy investment in them distracts us from what is important.	Checkout Ron Baker via www.verasage.com, LinkedIn or on his Amazon author page.

No.	Concept	Explanation	Story/source
9	100% is easy, 99% is hard	As soon as there are exceptions to any rule, the rule becomes virtually worthless. In other words, it is far easier to do something 100% of the time rather than any percentage less than that because any percentage less requires deep thought as to whether it is truly an exception to the rule.	Seth Godin is one of the strongest advocates of this concept.
10	UPOD	Under promise over deliver – whenever communicating with other team members, customers and referral sources, particularly in relation to time turnarounds, it is vital to take ownership of ensuring that a promise is understated and then do everything within your power to over deliver on the promise made.	A common theme in virtually every successful business is a culture of UPOD. Apple, for a sustained period, the world's most profitable firm, is a shining example.
11	Less is more	Jobs, among many others, is famous for understanding that a key to success in any area is making things as simple as possible; although not simpler (Einstein).	The foundation for this concept is arguably the quote 'Simplicity is the ultimate sophistication.' by Leonardo da Vinci
12	Never I	We are a customer centric organisation. Emails and letters that have every sentence starting with 'I' are not customer centric – indeed, it is preferable to never start any sentence with an 'I'.	101 principle, explained in detail by Simon Sinek in 'Start with Why' – i.e. your customers don't buy what you are doing, they buy why you are doing it.
13	Intraday communication	A business is founded on constant service delivery performance. Customers expect they are the only people in our lives, and we should therefore do whatever it takes, either directly or via other members of the team, to respond to every phone call and email intraday, even if it means outside 'normal' hours.	There are systems and tools including the AutoTextMe (Windows based) and Typeit4me (Apple based) that make this very simple to abide by.

No.	Concept	Explanation	Story/source
14	ATM is the answer	ATM stands for AutoTextMe. It is the tool that allows us to send emails that are pre-settled virtually instantaneously. In an ideal world, all aspects of communication in our business would be centralised in an ATM. Before then, we should simply use it as often as possible.	ATM is a stepping-stone to artificial intelligence in the law - artificial intelligence is already here, it is just not yet evenly distributed (see William Gibson's work on this theme).
15	The 3 step work test (rule of 1/5/35)	The '3 step work test' is that in our business you can do whatever work you want as long as you can do it – (a) Faster than a computer; (b) Cheaper than an Indian; (c) For at least 35 hours a day. In other words, due to automation, outsourcing and accessing multiple time zones at once, we must focus on the areas where we add the most amount of value.	This concept interrelates with many other principles in this table, including AI is here, when in doubt, flick it out and have you checked (the back of) your iPhone?
16	Only as good as the next job	While this is often used as a sports catch phrase, it is arguably derived from farming and gardening – i.e. it does not matter how well you have performed on a farm in a previous year – it is irrelevant if that same level of performance (or even better) is not attained in the following year.	Countless successful people and businesses have this as one of their key mantras. When embraced with other concepts in this table such as MVP, failing fast and UPOD, this concept is vital.

No.	Concept	Explanation	Story/source
17	AAR	AAR stands for after action review. It is a critical KPI for our business and has been inspired by both VeraSage and the military. It is a without fault review for the purposes of capturing our intellectual property and improving in the future.	The best source is probably Ron Baker's work through VeraSage and his various books.
18	Honour those absent	Talking about people, whether they are members of our team, customers or anyone else behind their back, in a way that does not honour their presence is a cancerous activity.	Again, reference Covey's '7 Habits of Highly Effective People.'
19	Start with why	Most people and organisations start by focusing on what they do and leave their why to the very end of their thinking – or perhaps never get to it.

'Why' is in fact where we all need to start, and invariably, it is not a why focused on ourselves, rather a why focused on how other people feel and interact with the solutions that we provide. | See Simon Sinek's record breaking TEDx performance and his book of the same name. |
| 20 | 7 Habits of Highly Effective People | Essentially, every 'self-help' book is summarised into this one publication. It was ground breaking when released and remains almost without peer. | Check out the Franklin Covey Institute and most of the books written by Stephen Covey. |
| 21 | Strengths focused activity leads to flow which leads to happiness | Common sense suggests that people should focus on their weaknesses to improve. Uncommon sense suggests that people should focus on their strengths. | Check out the internet in relation to the concept of 'flow' and the Gallup Strength Finder platform. It helps people set themselves up for success in a way that no other platform allegedly offering insights seems able to achieve. |

No.	Concept	Explanation	Story/source
22	Apply uncommon sense	Common sense is not in fact common. Strive to apply uncommon sense.	This concept, like many in this table is easy to say and much more difficult to apply. It is easier to understand in the context of the concept that 'exercising good judgment comes from experience, and experience is derived from exercising bad judgment'.
23	Every book we handout is a seedling for our next big job	Books are still arguably the most sustaining and resonating form of marketing that there is. We have invested exceptionally heavily in our technical legal books, however for relatively nominal cost, we are able to have a permanent business card with everyone that we can legitimately sell or hand one to.	Andrew Griffiths is one of Australia's best ever selling authors and lives his life by the same mantra. Importantly, the investment we make to write these books improves our performance and skills immeasurably.
24	Disruptive innovation is an undeniable truth	Clayton Christensen has explained disruptive innovation for over two decades and our firm is founded in the belief that the legal industry is on the cusp of what has happened to countless other industries. We believe that if we are not disrupting our most profitable products with a cheaper, easier, IT driven solutions, then our competitors will be.	Steve Jobs said Christensen's work was the only business literature he paid any attention to, and the modern version of Apple is largely founded on Christensen's theories.
25	Write a book	There is a theory that every business founder should write at least one book explaining their vision.	The Dream Enabler is one example.

No.	Concept	Explanation	Story/source
26	Remember from where we have come	Most, possibly all, 'overnight success' is the result of years of disciplined commitment. Understanding this journey, particularly through story sharing, provides grounding for our success and inspires us to strive for the next step.	See Gladwell's books 'Outliers' and the '10,000 hour rule'.
27	What is the next step?	One of the biggest causes of problems such as Parkinson's Law is the inability to articulate the exact 'next step'. Simply defining the next step and agreeing who is accountable and by when can revolutionise a business.	Much of the thinking in this space is captured by the work of the Heath brothers – for example see their book 'Switch'.
28	Have you checked (the back of) your iPhone?	Two sentences, on the back of every iPhone, explain value exceptionally well. The two sentences are 'Designed in California. Assembled in China'.	The science underpinning this theory of value can be largely traced to the Stan Shih Smile Curve – see Google.
29	We grow with our customers	A very significant proportion of our business is sourced from either repeat customers or direct personal referrals from previous customers. This is the sign of a truly fantastic business and something that we should never let go of.	The strongest businesses are built off the back of personal referrals, and David Maister, the US consultant, encapsulates this best with his 'two rules of marketing'. Namely, first, never seek out a new customer until you have entirely serviced a current customer, and then the second rule is that – if you ever think you have satisfied rule one, try again.

No.	Concept	Explanation	Story/source
30	We are all predictably irrational	Behavioural economics is a centrepiece of our business model.	Dan Ariely is probably the leading thinker in this area. Check out any of his books or his famous 'TEDx presentation where he explains how simply adding a third price point (the Goldilocks effect) can radically change the choices that a person makes.
31	Finish what you start	Our 'ping' society sets us up for failure in terms of completing one task at a time. No person, regardless of their age or gender can multitask. Finishing any task means not doing a single other task until the agreed job is entirely complete. No email checking. No phone calls. No social media. No grabbing a coffee. Do. What. Is. Needed. To. Ship.	The science behind interruption to a task is that it normally takes around 20 minutes for a person's brain to get back to where they were at the point of interruption.
32	Just Ship It	'Shipping' is the concept that our customers are only interested in the service being delivered to them – i.e. the product shipped. Embracing this mantra also means rejecting ideas such as time billing.	Seth Godin explains this concept.
33	We rage against the machine	While the phase is perhaps best known as the name of the influential US rock band, our business is founded on not accepting the status quo (no band name pun intended).	Our business plan embraces this mantra via our 'old view V new view' table. See the extract of this at the end of this table.

No.	Concept	Explanation	Story/source
34	Find the choke point	Like AAR's, this is another concept borrowed from the military. Our business success depends on working out where the most important issues for our customers are – and focusing our skills to creating innovative fixes. We similarly focus on solving the choke points in our own business.	A longstanding principle in military that has been used with success in gaming and business alike.
35	More with less	We define innovation in four words – doing more with less.	This concept is perhaps the most embraced definition of innovation. Two famous books in the space are 'The Toilet Paper Entrepreneur' by Mike Michalowicz and 'Frugal Innovation: How to Do More with Less' by Navi Radjou and Jaideep Prabhu
36	Gamification	A growing theory across all aspects of life, gamification focuses on making systems, services and activities more enjoyable and motivating.	We have been fortunate to see the work in this area by one leading thinker Clinton Swaine – see - http://www.frontiertrainings.com/
37	KISS is good	'Keeping it simple stupid' is a fundamental concept that we benchmark back to wherever possible.	While this is a common theme, arguably the best story is the 'toothpaste box' story by Cliff Williams. See the extract of this at the end of this table.
38	B1G1	B1G1 is the community focused charitable organisation that allows our business to regularly contribute to communities less fortunate than our own.	The chairman of B1G1 is Paul Dunn – he co-wrote with Ron Baker 'Firm of the Future' and has been a mentor for many businesses for many years. The concept of regularly giving small amounts to form a habit and not wasting huge sums on administrative overheads resonates with the way we do business.

No.	Concept	Explanation	Story/source
39	Entrepreneurship is not negotiable	Our success is derived from entrepreneurial customers. We have no choice other than to be entrepreneurial ourselves.	Leading thinkers such as Richard Branson, Warren Buffett, Anita Roddick, Jeff Bezos, Scroo and Jude Turner are famous examples of this theme.
40	Equality of opportunity, not outcome	All successful firms are based on the concept of giving everyone an opportunity, not guaranteeing some sort of equality of outcome.	Check out what happened to Marxism and socialism where communities and businesses were focused on equality of outcome.
41	Differing views are fostered	The different perspectives we all bring are critical to the ongoing growth and sustainability of our business.	When two people in business constantly think the same way, one of them is surplus to requirements.
42	We only ever want one person accountable	Organisations that start setting up committees for making decisions create inertia and bureaucracy that ultimately destroy the firm.	Look at any organisation that has embraced concepts such as the 2-pizza rule used by Amazon, Gore's rule of 150, Flight Centre micro teams and Apple 'skunkworks'.
43	Unconscious bias	There are a vast array of common biases around concepts such as affinity bias, interest bias, pattern recognition and gender. We need to foster a culture to allow all of us to become self-aware.	Google 'unconscious bias' and there are plenty of hits.
44	Technical excellence is simply the ticket to the event	We, and in turn our customers, simply expect exceptional technical excellence. This is not a differentiator itself, however it means that we must all commit to significant professional development each and every week.	Commit to a training program of self-education and learning, which you achieve every week.

No.	Concept	Explanation	Story/source
45	Everything needs to be four-eyed	Risks both in terms of technical content and commercial aspects can only be addressed where a second person reviews what you do. Take every available opportunity to have another review what you do and build the systems and processes to make them feel as though they are out of the job (i.e. they rarely ever find corrections).	There is significant science on this issue – intuitively, we know it firsthand when Murphy's Law (a derivative of Murphy's Law) takes over and sees a mistake sneak out in the one instance where a four-eye was not performed.
46	Print anything that is even remotely important	It is impossible to see errors and problems on an electronic screen. Anything of importance should be printed and methodically read on hardcopy.	Again, there is significant science around this concept.
47	Problem shared is a problem halved	Whenever there is anything that is troubling you, find the way to share the issue. It is rare that someone else in our firm will not have had to worry about the same thing before. Even where there is no internal knowledge, invariably someone will have a lead to contacts outside the firm that can help.	101 principle, which has in recent years been reinforced by significant scientific research.
48	Our success depends on IP centralisation	The ongoing disruptive nature of our business means that unless we can centralise and systemise everything that we do to ultimately automate it, we will not survive. It is imperative for all of us to take the extra time at the end of any task that might possibly be performed again to centralise that IP and to continue to build our precedents and knowledge bank.	Another aspect of Clayton Christensen's theory of disruptive innovation.

No.	Concept	Explanation	Story/source
49	Confidentiality is non-negotiable	It is absolutely critical that we maintain complete confidentiality in relation to all customer related aspects of our business. It is impossible to over emphasise the importance of confidentiality and the concept should be considered in the widest possible terms even to the extent of sharing information internally within the firm about particular customer scenarios.	101 principle, underpinned by the rule 100% is easy, 99% is hard.
50	We are part of a professional community	We have a fantastic network of other advisers who we can leverage off whenever needed. If something is too hard, again we should look to reach out to these advisers.	Centralise a list of those in your network who are part of your community. The 'problem shared is a problem halved' mantra is an adjacent concept.
51	It's not meant to be hard	We have a standing mantra to test why something is getting bogged down. Great solutions are regularly provided by intelligent workarounds.	This concept is another iteration of concepts in this table such as shipping, MVP, KISS and failing fast.
52	Is there another way?	Adjacent to the 'it's not meant to be hard' mantra is the mantra 'is there another way? Invariably, the newest members of our firm are the ones best able to help with this goal.	The most successful organisations are not wedded to processes and systems long since superseded. Perhaps the most often shared parable is the 'leg of ham' story. See the extract at the foot of this table.
53	1969 is the answer	Any feedback, particularly in the technology space, along the lines of - 'oh that can't be done', will generally be met with '1969' as the response.	Why is 1969 the answer? –Because that is when the moon landing occurred. If the technology existed in 1969 to allow the landing on the moon, everything is possible.

No.	Concept	Explanation	Story/source
54	If you think of it, it exists	The reality with our world is that if you can think of it, it either already exists; or will shortly.	Fundamental principle and one that Google answers instantaneously … try to Google something and not get answers, or at least leads to answers.
55	You're the voice	Our vocal health and delivery goes to the heart of our message. We invest heavily in vocal training.	We have been fortunate to learn from one of the leading thinkers in this area, Torb Pedersen. See his TEDx and – www.torbpedersen.com
56	Ass U me	When we assume something to be the case it makes an 'ass of you and me'.	'Assume' is said to be derived from the Latin words 'ass,' 'u' and 'me'. Generally it is accepted that, roughly translated, the word means 'to make an ass out of u and me'.
57	You are what you eat	Physical health begins and ends with food choices. We choose to eat real food, including starting each day with the now ubiquitous green smoothie.	The literature in this area is now overwhelming. For many the journey to learning in modern times was via Don Tolman – see www.dontolman.com
58	Every night is opening night	Similar, yet different, to the concept of only being as good as your next job. The key here is understanding that in every situation you are on show, even if you may have performed the 'same' content countless times before.	While a longstanding theory in theatre and performance, the principle also is critical from a risk perspective. Most mistakes in our business are the result of cutting corners and making assumptions.
59	Dress to impress	We embrace Richard Branson's 'Bye to the Tie'. We also understand that ideally in any environment it is preferable to have a dress standard comparable to the best dressed in the room.	The key to these themes link into the KISS theory. Arguably the most successful and productive individuals in history wear simple clothes that are essentially the same every day. This approach avoids wasting mental energy on (comparatively) unimportant questions.

No.	Concept	Explanation	Story/source
60	IP is meant to be free	Intellectual property, in the digital age, is meant to be freely available. We embrace this across all aspects of our business, with our articles, books, podcast channel, smart phone and tablet apps, webinars and seminars a few examples.	The Ron Baker quote on this concept is – 'If I give away my IP I have to replenish it. It keeps me at the constant edge.'
61	There is no such thing as work-life balance	The concept of trying to balance work and life as if they are separate concepts is nonsense. We embrace roles and opportunities in a way that allows people to play to their strengths and achieve a satisfying level of integration between what they do get paid for and the parts of their life where they are not getting paid. As we only die once, life is about 'getting on and hanging on'.	See increasing literature in this area, including 'Eat, move, sleep' by Tom Rath. Baker is more direct when he says – 'This concept of stressing work-life balance is pure poppycock. It is just a concept that says people want an excuse to be slackers. What people really need isn't more balance but more extremes. People simply require a passionate reason to bust their butt on or for something and then to go play just as hard.'
62	ROWE	We are a 'results only work environment' - not interested in form filling performance reviews or completing timesheets to prove how 'hard' we might have worked. The product of our application is the only criteria that we measure.	Google 'ROWE' for more information around this concept.
63	We spend equal time working on the business as in the business	We embrace the fact that our firm is a business and that it is critical to have key members 'off the legal tools' and thinking about how to be more relevant to our customers.	A rolling 90-day cycle built off the back of the 'Rockefeller Habits' (see Verne Harnish) is the centrepiece of our philosophy in this regard.

No.	Concept	Explanation	Story/source
64	Triple F	We believe that the work environment should be flexible and fun and create flow. It is the responsibility of each person to take personal ownership of achieving this outcome each and every day. If there are people that you work with that you believe are preventing you attaining this outcome, raise it with them directly, and immediately (i.e. same day) when the issue arises.	Again, refer to Covey.
65	And; not or	Historically businesses have focused on making 'or decisions' – i.e. doing one thing and not doing the other. Modern businesses need to find ways to embrace 'and'. Our business has done that by (for example) embracing both high-end quality specialist advice and our online delivery solutions.	See the book 'Doing Both' by head of strategy at Cisco – Inder Sidhu.
66	WWW	Finish every day with sharing with someone important to you 'what went well' that day personally and work wise.	See Adam Fraser's book, 'The Third Space'.
67	MVP is key (The 1/1/90 rule)	Getting a minimal viable product out into the market is the only way to test an idea. If you are not embarrassed by what is released, then you have released too late. We achieve this by having a priority (i.e. 1 of 1) goal that is shipped within 90 days.	See the book – The Lean Start Up.
68	Healthy brains are carried by healthy bodies	It is impossible to deliver in our space unless all physical and mental health is A grade. Exercise and eating real food (i.e. nothing processed) sets you up for success.	See the vast amount of literature available in this area including Tom Rath and Don Tolman (both mentioned elsewhere in this table).

No.	Concept	Explanation	Story/source
69	Move everyday	We have embraced concepts such as a stand-up desk and walking machines at work since the mid-2000s. Do whatever it takes to ensure that you are not sitting down for any extended periods, even in customer meetings.	Google stand-up desks, a concept we have embraced since 2007 and the science around 'walking meetings'.
70	Micro mentoring	We invest heavily in sharing and helping each of us achieve the key habits for success. We are not interested in constant check-ins about how workflow is progressing – we expect each person to be accountable for their business with the ultimate goal that each team member is tooled as quickly as possible to be in a situation where they could in fact establish their own business successfully.	See any of Gary Hamel's work.
71	Hang out with 5 people each day that are better than you	Your success will be determined by the people that you spend time with, even if it is simply by reading books by legendary thinkers. Make the effort every day to ensure that you have learnt something from at least 5 people smarter than you.	101 principle embraced by behavioural economics and made famous by Jim Rohn and his quote 'You are the average of the five people you spend the most time with'.
72	Manage your energy, not your time	Particularly with your hardest jobs, ensure that your energy levels are appropriate to allow completion.	Harvard has released a detailed article on this concept – see - https://hbr.org/2007/10/manage-your-energy-not-your-time
73	Diminishing returns	With every task, there is a point where after deliberate and considerate investment; your learning will start to significantly drop off. Be alive to this concept on every job and share a problem or roadblock as soon as the diminishing returns start setting in.	101 principle that links in with other concepts in this table such as managing energy, fail fast, shipping and the 4 eye policy.

No.	Concept	Explanation	Story/source
74	We are still passionate about time	While we do not track time spent on a task, we religiously track time to shipping – i.e. the duration that it has taken between receipt of instructions and delivery of end product.	Ron Baker's work captures most of the themes in this regard.
75	Make time for thinking	Some form of meditation style thinking is required every day. If you are not into formal meditation, find a substitute – for example, the moving meditation offered by swimming.	Google meditation for a few leads.
76	Routine is everything	Having a disciplined routine frees up brain space and creates habits. Most successful people have exceptionally disciplined routines that they follow at all times, including down to wearing the exact same clothes every day.	101 principle that links in with other concepts in this table such as dress to impress, zero inbox, checklists are everything and B1G1.
77	McDonald's marketing	Our business is founded on the original McDonald's model (not the iteration that it has now become) – i.e. delivering one core product and being super famous for it. On the back of that product, we then upsell immediately adjacent products. For McDonald's, that was the basic range of hamburgers and then upselling into a soft drink, fries and dessert. For us, our core product is our estate planning solution and then our adjacent products are the tax planning, asset protection, structuring etc.	Check out any McDonald's store, but in doing so, download off the internet a copy of their menu from 15 years ago and compare it to what they have done now.
78	Zero inbox	Each day should finish with there being zero items in the inbox. This is a big risk issue. If necessary, a separate 'to-do' or 'action' folder should be used.	See the book titled 'Zero Inbox' and various literature that sits around that via Google.

No.	Concept	Explanation	Story/source
79	Leverage the team to manage emails	All emails should be typed directly into your drafts folder by a typing team. Once you have settled them, the email should be separately moved into an 'emails for sending' folder and your admin team should send these.	See Tim Ferriss' The 4-Hour Workweek for extensive tips on working smarter, not harder.
80	Be vigilant with equipment and material	There are countless horror stories of, for example, children getting a hold of electronic equipment or staff accidentally leaving material somewhere that have caused significant damage to customers and business. Be vigilant and methodical in your safeguards in this area.	There are daily examples, if not hourly, of situations where a lack of attention in this area causes untold damage.
81	Thinking that got us here won't get us there	The ideas and solutions that have worked in the past for historical problems are unlikely to be of use for new problems.	See the book of the same name by Marshall Goldsmith and Mark Reiter.
82	The world is flat	The start of the end of many industries (including 'Big Law') was arguably back in the 1990s when the concept of a global workforce first materialised. We are constantly looking to embrace this framework still many years later.	Have a look at the book 'The World is Flat' and some related literature.
83	Think fast and slow	The literature in relation to the way our brains work and the seminal work 'Thinking Fast and Slow' is critical to understand in relation to our customers and also ourselves.	See the book 'Thinking Fast and Slow' by Noble Prize winner Daniel Kahneman

No.	Concept	Explanation	Story/source
84	Stay young, stay foolish	As mentioned in the foreword, this idea is derived from a quote often used by Steve Jobs, being to 'stay hungry, stay foolish.' The concept is that (similar to the mantra that 'only the paranoid survive') unless you are constantly enthusiastic for the future and keep your mind 'child like' in terms of being open to new ideas, you will be unsuccessful.	See Steve Jobs' TEDx Commencement address to Stanford University and the book 'Only the Paranoid Survive' by Andrew Grove.
85	Everything is borrowed	The classic quote is that 'good artists borrow, great artists steal.' We embrace this mantra.	The key point to understand is that the 'borrowing' is not from within the industry we operate; rather it is from across industry. The classic Apple example is the magnetised power cord they use for laptops – taken from the toaster industry in Japan.
86	We have no customers	We pride ourselves on being solely 'business to business' in our value proposition. This means that we never really have any customers at all – we treat our referral sources as if they were customers in a marketing sense. This also explains why we virtually never make referrals to other professionals – e.g. if an accountant refers a customer to us, no one will be interested in us then trying to refer that customer to a different accountant.	Our passion around finding other ways to deliver value back into our referral sources (for example, books, seminars, training, the entire VW (View Wholesale) model etc.) is partly driven by the fact that we have very limited cross referral opportunities.
87	Sanity is preserved via version control	Being methodical with version control goes to the heart of our business. This means that with any document that is being amended, it is vital to save it into a new version, accept any existing redline and then always amend in redline.	While common for many, there are a surprising number of people who either don't know, or choose not to use, redline changes – be aware and be prepared.

No.	Concept	Explanation	Story/source
88	Fail fast	All leading firms find a way to get products to market quickly, make the errors that are always made, then even more rapidly fix those errors and iterate the product so that it is attractive to a customer. Some argue the difference between success and failure can largely be determined by the time delays between conceptualising a product or improvement and getting that product or improvement into the market.	Google 'failing fast'.
89	We double our chances of having great team members with one simple strategy	We believe talent is not determined by gender; unlike the vast majority of law firms that are lucky to have a double-digit percentage of female leaders.	See the book 'Lean In' and significant related material.
90	21 tips for young players	There is a famous list of 21 ideas for success by H Jackson Brown that is always a timely reminder.	See http://www.21suggestions.com/
91	Brain food	Piecing together a summary of the most influential books and articles you read is a key to success.	Among countless others, Bill Gates attributes much of his success to this approach and an annual sabbatical when 'condensed' reading is done (i.e. reading multiple books in a short timeframe).

No.	Concept	Explanation	Story/source
92	Checklists are everything	A lot of our thinking behind the importance of checklists is set out in our 'checklist manifesto platform'. There is also an amazing amount of literature around two quite starkly different treks to the summit of Everest some years ago. The leader of one trek tragically perished, along with the majority of his group. The other group that suffered no casualties built their entire operation around checklists.	Read the books 'Into Thin Air' and 'Great by Choice' for a compelling and riveting summary of the various issues in relation the Everest treks. In 2015 a movie of the book 'Into Thin Air' was released. Also read the book – The Checklist Manifesto.
93	Get a coin toss app	With reference to some of the other line items above (including Thinking Fast and Slow), often the most important thing to do is to make a decision, rather than what the decision itself might be. A coin toss app helps solve many a dilemma. Use it earlier, use it often.	See the work of various behavioural thinkers, perhaps most famously the 3 Ds - Daniel Kahneman, Daniel Pink and Dan Ariely.
94	When in doubt, flick it out	With anything that you are considering the usefulness of delegating it or referring it, if you have to stop and think about whether it is the appropriate thing to do, then you are in doubt, and you should therefore flick it out.	101 principle that links in with other concepts in this table such as have you checked (the back of) your iPhone?, the 3 step work test and a problem shared is a problem halved.
95	We want our entire business runnable via our iPhones	Mobile is it. We need to find a way to ensure that every aspect of our business embraces a mobile centric solution.	Too many examples to list – although the revolution of Facebook about 18 months before it listed is arguably the most compelling.
96	Know your phone	In the context of the above line item, knowing as much about what your phone can do to leverage our business is the starting point.	See the extract at the end of this table.

No.	Concept	Explanation	Story/source
97	There is an app for that	Almost every issue we face has a solution of some description (often a near perfect answer) via a smart phone app.	The famous post by Steve Cichon from 2014 arguably best captures this concept. See the extract at the end of this table.
98	AI is here	Artificial Intelligence is rapidly becoming ubiquitous across all aspects of life. The provision of legal solutions will be drastically and irrecoverably changed by AI. We can 'get on and hang on' or choose some other game to play.	The literature in this space is overwhelming. Perhaps the simplest place to start is asking Siri on your iPhone if she/he is artificially intelligent. Odds on the response will be 'this is about you, not me'.
99	Rule of 7/11/4	This used to be the rule of 7 – i.e. it used to take 7 forms of interaction in a marketing sense for a referral source to be convinced to try us out. The number is now more like 7 hours of content, on 11 separate occasions, across 4 mediums. The trick is we never really will understand what things actually constitute a true interaction nor what referral sources place more emphasis on – hence our extremely broad and agnostic approach to all things marketing.	Marketing 101. Embrace it, while also referencing the seminal book 'How to Win Friends and Influence People' by Dale Carnegie. The rule of 7/11/4 is often attributed to Elon Musk.
100	Strategy is about no	True strategy is about saying no to things that are not completely aligned with where you are trying to get to.	Many have explained this model – perhaps most famously see David Maister's work or Apple's most successful solutions.
101	You only die once…	…so make sure it is worth it.	The quote is attributed to Vladimir Kama-risky. It captures in a sentence embracing the opportunities we are given, every single day.

Some Further Context

Section 2

KNOW YOUR PHONE

Your iPhone (smartphone) should enable you to do virtually everything that you need to do for work on a day-to-day basis.

This includes the following:

(1) You should never type anything yourself – typing has always been a race to the bottom and with complete voice recognition virtually here already, it is unsustainable.

(2) Find a fantastic typing team for anything longer than a couple of sentences.

(3) For things that are a couple of sentences long, you should use the 'Typeit4me' app that is the iPhone version of ATM.

(4) Alternatively, use the voice recognition program within the iPhone, or if necessary, Dragon (the free app works fine for short emails).

(5) The dictation app that we use is titled 'Dictate+ Connect'. It costs around $20.

(6) Tapes of up to around 1 hour can easily be sent automatically via your phone.

(7) The scanner pro app on your iPhone is best for scanning documents – you can normally get around 8 pages per email.

(8) For transport requirements, try to use public transport around the city and Uber where possible.

(9) When on the move, Dropbox allows access to a vast majority of material – for example, when presenting seminars.

(10) Similarly, the OWA app allows you to check your draft email account, even though the draft box does not show up on your handheld otherwise.

(11) From a risk and file maintenance perspective, try to get an admin team to send all the emails for you – simply setup a separate folder under your drafts folder and you can drag and drop approved emails into that folder and then arrange for the admin team to go through the mechanical exercise of sending and filing everything for you – just ensure that you BCC yourself on the email so that you know that it is gone.

(12) Due to the number of time zones many people work in every day, both around the country and then overseas, the 'time buddy' app is perfect for ensuring that we do not get confused between time zones. This is also very useful for setting up, for example, 'invites' for meetings across jurisdictions and webinars etc.

(13) The Pomodoro app is perfect for ensuring that there is no 'white noise' or interruptions when you are doing work. It provides rolling 25-minute blocks of countdowns to ensure that you do not, for example, check emails, take phone calls or otherwise distract yourself from the task at hand.

(14) You should also turn off all notifications on your phone so that the pings are not coming up on that in the same way as you turn off the notifications on your Outlook Surface environment.

(15) Whenever doing a particular task, it is ideal to do that 'offline' as well, so that you are at least not in Outlook and ideally not in front of your computer at all.

(16) Zoom on the handheld is a great app for video conferencing (or alternatively, Skype Business/Lync).

(17) You should also ensure that you have the iPhone find app enabled.

(18) Use a proper passcode (ideally thumb print) on your handheld devices.

(19) When you're creating an office environment on the move, use secure trusted locations for printing.

(20) Agreeadate.com allows you to easily schedule meetings with multiple parties.

THE TOOTHPASTE BOX STORY

A toothpaste factory had a problem.

They sometimes shipped empty boxes without the tube inside. This was caused by the way the production line was set up, and people with experience in designing production lines will tell you how difficult it is to have everything happen with timings so precise that every single unit coming out of it is perfect 100% of the time.

Small variations in the environment (which can't be controlled in a cost-effective fashion) mean you must have quality assurance checks smartly distributed across the line so customers all the way down to the supermarket don't get angry and buy another product instead.

Understanding how important that was, the CEO of the toothpaste factory got the top people in the company together and they decided to form a committee to start a new project in which they would hire an external engineering company to solve their empty boxes problem since their engineering department was already too stretched to take on any extra effort.

The project followed the usual process: budget and project sponsor allocated, RFP and third parties selected.

Six months (and $8 million) later, they had a fantastic solution - on time, on budget, high quality and everyone in the project had a great time. They solved the problem by using high-tech precision scales that would sound a bell and flash lights whenever a toothpaste box would weigh less than it should. The line would stop and someone would have to walk over and yank the defective box out of it, pressing another button when done to restart the line.

A while later, the CEO decides to have a look at the ROI of the project and sees amazing results! No empty boxes ever shipped out of the factory after the scales were put in place. There were very few customer complaints and they were gaining market share. 'That's some money well spent!', he says, before looking closely at the other statistics in the report.

It turns out the number of defects picked up by the scales was zero after three weeks of production use. It should have been picking up at least a dozen a day, so maybe there was something wrong with the report. He filed a bug against it and after some investigation, the engineers came back saying the report was actually correct. The scales really weren't picking up any defects because all boxes that got to that point in the conveyor belt were good.

Puzzled, the CEO travels down to the factory and walks up to the part of the line where the precision scales were installed.

A few feet before the scales was a $30 desk fan blowing the empty boxes off the belt and into a bin.

'Oh, that,' says one of the workers when asked by the CEO what the story was, 'one of the guys put it there 'cause he was tired of walking over every time the bell rang.'

THE LEG OF HAM STORY

The story is told of a woman who brought home a leg of ham and was preparing it for Christmas Dinner.

She proceeded to cut it in half, before placing it in the oven to cook it.

Her husband, watching on, asked 'Why did you cut the ham in half? Is that so it cooks better in the middle?'

His wife paused a moment and then answered 'I don't really know, that's just what I've always done. I saw my mother doing that when I was a girl'.

Later the wife's family arrived for Christmas dinner and the question was brought up again 'Mum – why do you cut the leg of ham in half before placing it in the oven to cook?'

'I don't really know', her mother replied. 'Your grandma used to do that – so it's just something I've always done – I am sure there must be a good reason for it!'

Later the family all travelled to Grandma's house to share Christmas tea.

During a lull in the conversation, the wife asked her grandmother, 'Grandma, why do you cut the leg of ham in half before cooking it?'

'I don't', came Grandma's response.

'But mum told me that's how she learnt to do it from you', the wife responded.

'Yes well that is probably correct', replied the grandmother, 'however when your mother was a young girl, my oven was very small and I couldn't fit the whole leg in without cutting it in half. That hasn't been a problem for years'.

THE VIEW BUSINESS PLAN

Why

To—

(1) fundamentally improve the value and experience of legal solutions by collaboratively leveraging our unique strengths

(2) build the kind of firm our friends would choose

(3) be the favourite advisers of those who engage us

How

This can be summarised in the following table (focus on View Legal column):

Old View	View Legal
Top single discipline legal talent	Legal talent with skills in adjacent areas including process management, IT and customer service
Key metric – annual full equity partner draws	Key metric – have we radically improved the ability to increase the value provided to customers
'Own' clients	Are trusted to serve customers
Bill clients on hourly rates (or various, increasingly elaborate, permutations on the theme) and give no guarantee as to client satisfaction	Customers provided up front 'SPS Guarantees' –that is service and price satisfaction is guaranteed
Everything tracked on a timesheet. The longer something takes, the better.	No timesheets. Sophisticated project management tools used to help ensure customer expectations are exceeded.
Quality is defined by the law firm	Quality is defined by the customer
'Impressive' CBD office space, with 'dominant' fit outs	View meets where best suits Customers. No permanent CBD space retained.
Intellectual property is how we make money and should be guarded jealously	Intellectual property is how we create trust and should be shared freely
Lawyers striving to deliver near-perfect technical excellence	All service designed to be fit-for-purpose, aligning with collaboratively agreed customer objectives
Lawyers expected to both find and produce work for clients	Business development and production of work separated, leveraging technology and worldwide resources
Lawyers focus on 'is this billable' for the firm	Lawyers focus on 'is this valuable' for the customer
Promotion of the personal brands of rainmakers	Promotion of the View brand
Use of sustaining technologies (i.e. Christensen 's Innovator's Dilemma) –this is the only way'	Application of disruptive technologies (again Christensen) –the View mantra is 'there must be another, smarter, way'

Old View	View Legal
'Leveraging' of full-time lawyers to do the bulk of the work serving clients	Flexible work practices that match supply with demand clients
Creation of a tournament to motivate lawyers to strive to become equity partners	No tournament, focus on collaboration across entire team
Tight restriction of the number of equity owners	Non-lawyer shareholders and all team members have access to equity returns
Structured or behave as a partnership	Incorporated
Constant focus on the 'need for diversity' of gender	Only focus on diversity of thought
Extensive management required of all lawyers and partners	Team self-selected which allows self-management and a results only work environment
Revenue growth the #1 goal	Exceeding customer expectations #1 goal

What

We embrace technology as an enabler to our business and we will look across and within industry to achieve best practice.

More specifically we:

Increase, as defined by customers	Decrease, as defined by customers	Abolish	Add
Value	Complexity	Heritage thinking	Entrepreneurship
Quality	Engagement friction	Arrogance	Young minds
Accessibility	Unnecessary overheads	Surprises	Humour

EVERYTHING FROM THE 1991 RADIO SHACK AD I NOW DO ON MY IPHONE

Some people like to spend $3 on a cup of coffee. While that sounds like a gamble I probably wouldn't take, I'll always like to gamble—especially as little as three bucks— on what I might be able to dig up on Buffalo and Western New York, our collective past, and what it means for our future.

I recently came across a big pile of Buffalo News front sections from 1991, every day for the first three months of the year… collected as the First Gulf War unfolded. $3. I probably could have chiselled the guy down a buck, but I happily paid to see what else was in those papers.

There's plenty about a run up to the first Super Bowl appearance ever for the Bills, and mixed in with the disappointment is an air of hope and expectation for what is to come. Harumph. There are also some great local ads commemorating and/or coat-tailing on the Bills success.

We'll get to those someday, but today, something much simpler. The back page of the front section on Saturday, February 16, 1991 was 4/5ths covered with a Radio Shack ad.

There are 15 electronic gizmo type items on this page, being sold from America's Technology Store. 13 of the 15 you now always have in your pocket.

So here's the list of what I've replaced with my iPhone.

- All weather personal stereo, $11.88. I now use my iPhone with an Otter Box
- AM/FM clock radio, $13.88. iPhone.
- In-Ear Stereo Phones, $7.88. Came with iPhone.
- Micro thin calculator, $4.88. Swipe up on iPhone.
- Tandy 1000 TL/3, $1599. I actually owned a Tandy 1000, and I used it for games and word processing. I now do most of both of those things on my phone.
- VHS Camcorder, $799. iPhone.
- Mobile Cellular Telephone, $199. Obvs.
- Mobile CB, $49.95. Ad says "You'll never drive 'alone' again!" iPhone.
- 20-Memory Speed-Dial phone, $29.95.
- Deluxe Portable CD Player, $159.95. 80 minutes of music, or 80 hours of music? iPhone.
- 10-Channel Desktop Scanner, $99.55. I still have a scanner, but I have a scanner app, too. iPhone.
- Easiest-to-Use Phone Answerer, $49.95. iPhone voicemail.
- Handheld Cassette Tape Recorder, $29.95. I use the Voice Memo app almost daily.
- BONUS REPLACEMENT: It's not an item for sale, but at the bottom of the ad, you're instructed to 'check your phone book for the Radio Shack Store nearest you.' Do you even know how to use a phone book?

You'd have spent $3054.82 in 1991 to buy all the the stuff in this ad that you can now do with your phone. That amount is roughly equivalent to about $5100 in 2012 dollars.

The only two items on the page that my phone really can't replace:

- Tiny Dual-Superheterodyne Radar Detector, $79.95. But when is the last time you heard the term "fuzz-buster" anyway?
- 3-Way speaker with massive 15" Woofer, $149.95.

It's nothing new, but it's a great example of the technology of only two decades ago now replaced by the 3.95-ounce bundle of plastic, glass, and processors in our pockets

Section 3

Quotes to Note

Success is what you attract by the person you become. –*Jim Rohn*

No can make you feel inferior without your permission. –*Eleanor Roosevelt*

The young do not know enough to be prudent, and therefore they attempt the impossible – and achieve it, generation after generation. –*Pearl S. Buck*

The conventional view serves to protect us from the painful job of thinking. –*John Kenneth Galbraith*

Formal education will make you a living; self-education will make you a fortune. –*Jim Rohn*

To earn more, you must learn more. –*Brian Tracy*

Give so much time to the improvement of yourself that you have no time to criticise others. –*Christian D. Larson*

Your life only gets better, when you get better! –*Brian Tracy*

The poor and middle class work for money. The rich have money work for them. –*Robert Kiyosaki*

Experience is what you get when you do not get what you want. –*Anonymous*

The biggest mistake we could ever make in our lives is to think we work for anybody but ourselves. –*Brian Tracy*

The surest way not to fail is to determine to succeed. –*Richard B. Sheridan*

Try not to become a man of success, but try rather to become a man of value. –*Albert Einstein.*

There is always a philosophy for lack of courage. –*Albert Camus*

Every company has room for the man who has a definite plan of action, which is to the advantage of that company. –*Napoleon Hill*

It's not what you have, it's what you do with what you have. –*Anonymous*

It matters not what a person is born, but who they choose to be. –*Joanne Kathleen Rowling*

Most misfortunes are the result of misused time. –*Napoleon Hill*

We don't see things the way they are. We see things the way we are. –*Talmud*

Employ your time in improving yourself by other men's writings so that you shall come easily by what others have laboured hard for. –*Socrates*

The price of excellence is discipline. The cost of mediocrity is disappointment. –*William Arthur Ward*

Don't worry about people stealing your ideas. If your ideas are any good, you'll have to ram them down people's throats. –*Howard Aiken*

A quitter never wins and a winner never quits. –*Napoleon Hill*

If you want to go somewhere, it is best to find someone who has already been there. –*Robert Kiyosaki*

We are what we repeatedly do. Excellence, therefore, is not an act but a habit. –*Aristotle*

The best way out is always through. –*Robert Frost*

Do not wait to strike till the iron is hot; but make it hot by striking. –*William B. Sprague*

Great spirits have always encountered violent opposition from mediocre minds. –*Albert Einstein*

Whether you think you can or think you can't, you're right. –*Henry Ford*

I know for sure that what we dwell on is who we become. –*Oprah Winfrey*

I've missed more than 9000 shots in my career. I've lost almost 300 games. 26 times, I've been trusted to take the game winning shot and missed. I've failed over and over and over again in my life. And that is why I succeed. –*Michael Jordan*

Failure is an option here. If things are not failing, you are not innovating enough. –*Elon Musk*

The first step is to establish that something is possible; then probability will occur. –*Elon Musk*

You want to be extra rigorous about making the best possible thing you can. Find everything that's wrong with it and fix it. Seek negative feedback, particularly from friends. –*Elon Musk*

You must be the change you want to see in the world. –*Mahatma Gandhi*

Your time is limited, so don't waste it living someone else's life. –*Steve Jobs*

What you get by achieving your goals is not as important as what you become by achieving your goals. –*Goethe*

You can get everything in life you want if you will just help enough other people get what they want. –*Zig Ziglar*

You have brains in your head. You have feet in your shoes. You can steer yourself, any direction you choose. –Dr Seuss

Do or do not. There is no try. –Yoda

Empty pockets never held anyone back. Only empty heads and empty hearts can do that. –Norman Vincent Peale

Always go to other people's funerals, otherwise they won't come to yours. –Yogi Berra

When you come to a fork in the road, take it! –Yogi Berra

If you don't know where you are going, you'll end up someplace else. –Yogi Berra

The future 'ain't what it used to be. –Yogi Berra

Cut my pie into four pieces, I don't think I could eat eight. –Yogi Berra

In theory, there is no difference between theory and practice. But in practice, there is. –Yogi Berra

Nobody comes here anymore, it's too crowded. –Yogi Berra

Déjà vu, all over again. –Yogi Berra

We made too many wrong mistakes. –Yogi Berra

I'd give my right arm to be ambidextrous. –Yogi Berra

We're lost, but we're making good time. –*Yogi Berra*

You wouldn't have won if we'd beaten you. –*Yogi Berra*

It's tough to make predictions, especially about the future. –*Yogi Berra*

All truth passes through three stages. First, it is ridiculed. Second, it is violently opposed. Third, it is accepted as being self-evident. –*Arthur Schopenhauer*

Success is the ability to survive your mistakes. –*George Rathman*

At high altitudes even the smartest companies are not immune to dizziness and groupthink. –*Jim Champy*

Everyone is a genius. But if you judge a fish by its ability to climb a tree, it will spend its whole life believing it is stupid. –*Einstein*

Any fool can criticise, condemn and complain – and most fools do. –*Benjamin Franklin*

When in danger or in doubt run in circles, scream and shout. –*Robert Heinlein*

Our greatest glory is not in never failing, but in rising every time we fail. –*Confucius*

I can't understand why people are frightened of new ideas – I am frightened of the old ones. –*John Cage*

The young are always in the right, because time is on their side. And that means we have to change. –*Peter Drucker*

When two people in business always agree, one of them is unnecessary. –*William Wrigley*

A successful man is one who can lay a firm foundation with the bricks others have thrown at him. –*David Brinkley*

In the choice between changing one's mind and proving there is no need to do so, most people get busy on the proof. –*John Kenneth Galbraith*

The intuitive mind is a sacred gift and a rational mind is a faithful servant. We have created a society that honours the servant and has forgotten the gift. –*Albert Einstein*

Common sense is a curious name for something so rare. –*Mark Twain*

Building a better scale does not change your weight. In other words, measurement for measurement sake is senseless, furthermore lead indicators are infinitely more valuable than lag indicators. –*Philip Crosby*

But while my inner voice was clearly telling me I was at my core an entrepreneur, it's inconvenient to decide at twenty-three that you can't really work for other people. –*Kelly Cutrone*

Winning isn't everything, but wanting to win is. –*Vince Lombardi*

Certainly, Franklin said Time is money. He was not speaking of value or price, however, he was simply explaining the concept of opportunity cost – i.e. that every activity or product in the economy has an alternative use. –*Paul Dunn and Ron Baker*

It is theory, which decides what we can observe. –*Albert Einstein*

Eighty percent of success is showing up. –*Woody Allen*

The purpose of a business is to innovate and create wealth for its customers (not simply to be efficient). *–Peter Drucker*

The purpose of business is to create and keep a customer. *–Peter Drucker*

Innovation is the specific instrument of entrepreneurship…the act that endows resources with a new capacity to create wealth. *–Peter Drucker*

The great thing about lead indicators is that every employee can influence the outcome of each of them. *–Paul Dunn and Ron Baker*

You must however define success in the way that your customers define it – most businesses fail because they say they want the right things, but then measure and reward the wrong things. *–Ron Baker*

Total quality management (TQM) is doomed to failure because the efforts begin as administrative, analytical, mechanical, control oriented, dehumanising, standard space management attempts in order to tighten up the organisation rather than loosen it up and empower the firm's people to make their own individual quality commitments. *–Albrecht*

People often say that motivation doesn't last. Well, neither does bathing. That's why we recommend it daily. *–Zig Ziglar*

There is never a right way to do the wrong thing – nothing is so useless as doing efficiently that which should not be done at all. *–Peter Drucker*

An organisation can internally count, measure and analyse against almost any standard, but weighing yourself 10 times a day will not reduce your weight. *–Peter Drucker*

Quality is not the absence of defects as defined by management, it is the presence of value as defined by customers. *–Peter Drucker*

There's an old saying in business: What gets measured is what gets done. What's happening today is the flip side of that. Measurement has become a tyranny that makes sure that nothing gets done. *–Thomas Dee*

Any measurement is always going to require judgment, otherwise manipulating numbers will become more important than creating value for customers. *–Peter Drucker*

A persons worth to an organisation can be measured by the amount of supervision they require. *–Jim Casey*

The resources wasted cloaked under the names of benchmarking and best practices are extraordinary, particularly given that they are normally done at the expense of investing in R&D and experimenting with innovation. *–Ron Baker*

Early to bed, early to rise, work like hell, and advertise. *–Ted Turner*

I am not a product of my circumstances. I am a product of my decisions. *–Stephen Covey*

Benchmarking is not a way to build a strategic advantage. The professions spend almost all of their time gazing at each other's navels rather than finding ways to change the rules of the game. *–Ron Baker*

Saying no to loud people gives you the resources to say yes to important opportunities. *–Seth Godin*

Successful people are the ones who are breaking the rules. *–Seth Godin*

If you spend your life trying to be good at everything, you will never be great at anything. *–Tom Rath*

You can never know how to do something you have never done before, otherwise there could be no innovation. *–Ron Baker*

The fundamental problem with benchmarking studies is that they focus on the results of a process, not the process itself. They tend to confuse the cause and effect – the cause is hidden, the effect is visible to all. *–Ovid*

It's unwise to pay too much, but it's worse to pay too little. When you pay too much, you lose a little money – that's all. When you pay too little, you sometimes lose everything, because the thing you bought was incapable of doing the thing it was bought to do. *–John Ruskin*

The best swordsman in the world does not need to fear the second best swordsman. The person for him to be afraid of is some ignorant antagonist who has never had a sword in his hand before, does not do the thing he ought to do and therefore the expert is not prepared for him, does not do what he ought to do and often the expert is then caught out and is ended on the spot. *–Mark Twain*

The two most important days in your life are the day you are born and the day you find out why. *–Mark Twain*

I've learned that people will forget what you said, people will forget what you did, but people will never forget how you made them feel. *–Maya Angelou*

Would you like me to give you a formula for success? It's quite simple, really: Double your rate of failure. You are thinking of failure as the enemy of success. But it isn't at all. You can be discouraged by failure or you can learn from it, so go ahead and make mistakes. Make all you can. Because remember that's where you will find success. —*Thomas Watson*

Always forgive your enemies. Nothing annoys them more. —*Oscar Wilde*

Until people are mocking you, you are not repeating your message enough. —*Verne Harnish*

Focus groups are for losers. —*Steve Jobs*

Steve Jobs gave a small private presentation about the iTunes Music Store to some independent record label people. My favourite line of the day was when people kept raising their hand saying, "Does it do [x]?", "Do you plan to add [y]?".

Finally Jobs said, "Wait wait – put your hands down. Listen: I know you have a thousand ideas for all the cool features iTunes could have. So do we. But we don't want a thousand features. That would be ugly. Innovation is not about saying yes to everything. It's about saying NO to all but the most crucial features. —*Derek Sivers*

Consensus is the absence of Leadership. It is the process of abandoning all beliefs, principles, values and policies in search of something in which no one believes, but to which no one objects; the process of avoiding the very issues that have to be solved, merely because you cannot get agreement on the way ahead. What great cause would have been fought and won under the banner I stand for consensus? —*Margaret Thatcher*

It does not require a majority to prevail, but rather an irate, tireless minority keen to set bush fires in people's minds. –*Samuel Adams*

I skate to where the puck is going to be, not to where it has been. –*Wayne Gretzky*

You miss 100 percent of the shots you don't take. –*Wayne Gretzky*

Flawless execution cannot compensate for implementing the wrong solution. –*Daryl Conner*

When the rate of change outside exceeds the rate of change inside, the end is in sight. –*Jack Welch*

The problem is not how to get new thoughts into your mind, but how to get the old ones out. –*Nancy Austin*

There is nothing more difficult to take in hand, more perilous to conduct, or more uncertain in success than to take the lead in the introduction of a new order of things. –*Machiavelli*

It is not the strongest of the species who survive, nor the most intelligent, but the ones most responsive to change. –*Charles Darwin*

Character cannot be developed in ease and quiet. Only through experience of trial and suffering can the soul be strengthened, ambition inspired, and success achieved. –*Helen Keller*

It is a simple task to make things complex, but a complex task to make them simple. –*Meyers Law*

The way to get started is to quit talking and begin doing. –*Walt Disney*

The illiterate of the 21st century will not be those who cannot read and write, but those who cannot learn, unlearn and relearn. –*Alvin Toffler*

If a man voices his opinion in a forest and no woman hears him, is he still wrong? –*Anonymous*

Anyone who believes that exponential growth can go on forever in a finite world is either a madman or an economist. –*Kenneth Boulding*

Why did God invent economists? – To make weathermen feel good about themselves. –*David Rosenberg*

If you want to change the fruits, you will first have to change the roots. If you want to change the visible, you must first change the invisible. –*T. Harv Eker*

Dear Karma, I have a list of some of the people you missed. –*Anonymous*

Ever noticed how those whose typical Friday night involves driving home in a German car, wearing an Italian suit, stopping to buy a Belgian beer, at a Dubai owned shopping mall, phoning on a Korean made smartphone, designed in Sweden, for Indian takeaway to spend an evening sitting on Indonesian furniture, watching American programs on a Chinese made TV are then against offshoring as its unAustralian and they are suspicious of anything foreign. –*Anonymous*

If you don't cannibalize yourself, somebody else will. –*Steve Jobs*

The job of art is to chase ugliness away. –*Bono*

There are no secrets to success. It is the result of preparation, hard work, and learning from failure. –*Colin Powell*

You know you are on the road to success if you would do your job, and not be paid for it. –*Oprah Winfrey*

Eating at Steve's (Jobs) is fine as long as you get out before the local restaurants close. –*Rupert Murdoch*

The best and most innovative products don't always win. –*Steve Jobs*

People do judge a book by its cover. –*Steve Jobs*

Simplicity is the ultimate sophistication. –*da Vinci*

Good artists copy, great artists steal. –*Picasso*

There is a shadow between conception and creation. –*TS Eliot*

Great art stretches the taste, it doesn't follow tastes. –*Steve Jobs*

What's the difference between Apple and boy scouts – boy scouts have adult supervision. –*Steve Jobs*

I am so old I can remember when other people's achievements were considered an inspiration not a grievance. –*Thomas Sowell*

In life there are only two things, results and reasons. Successful people have lots of results and unsuccessful people have lots of reasons. –*Keith J. Cunningham*

My living will –

Last night, my kids and I were sitting in the living room and I said to them,

I never want to live in a vegetative state, dependent on some machine and fluids from a bottle. If that ever happens, just pull the plug.

They got up, unplugged the computer and threw out my wine!!

The little so & so's –Anonymous

Behind every great man there is a surprised woman. –Maryon Pearson

I feel so miserable without you around – it's almost like having you here. –Stephen Bishop

When I am right I get angry. When he gets angry he's wrong. You often end up angry at each other. –Charles De Gaulle

He was happily married – but his wife wasn't. –Victor Borge

Success seems to be connected with action. Successful people keep moving. They make mistakes, but they don't quit. –Conrad Hilton

Shut up and move on. –Sumo

Rich people have big libraries poor people have big TVs. –Jim Rohn

Divorce – Debit experience, Credit net wealth. –Ron Baker

The test of a first rate intelligence is the ability to hold two opposed ideas in the mind at the same time and still retain the ability to function. –F Scott Fitzgerald

Never, ever, ever be as good as you're going to be. –Joe Calloway

Logic will get you from A to B. Imagination will take you everywhere. –Albert Einstein

Having a high IQ is proof of the ability to get a higher score on an IQ test and possibly a few other things although it's uncertain exactly what those are. –Karl Albrecht

One of the biggest impediments to learning is the belief that you already know everything. That assumption makes you lose your beginners mind which is sensitive to all sorts of possibilities in favour of an expert mind, which is narrow and conformist. –Nassim Nicholas Taleb

A man convinced against his will is of the same opinion still. –William Blake

The successful warrior is the average man, with laser-like focus. –Bruce Lee

Change your thoughts and you change your world. –Norman Vincent Peale

In our saner moments we realise that we tend to get better results in dealing with most people and most situations by approaching them in a positive cooperative spirit rather than an antagonistic spirit. –Karl Albrecht

Arguing rarely changes anyone's mind; it just leads to more arguing. –Karl Albrecht

By commonly accepted definitions of addiction, the experience of watching TV on a regular basis is addictive – not in a figurative, joking sense but in a real, literal and clinical sense. –*Karl Albrecht*

Keep on going, and the chances are that you will stumble on something, perhaps when you are least expecting it. I never heard of anyone ever stumbling on something sitting down. –*Charles F. Kettering*

The best way to get what you want is to be sure the other person is getting what they want. –*Joe Calloway*

When you have exhausted all possibilities, remember this: You haven't. –*Thomas Edison*

The great disadvantage of experience is the loss of the stupidity and absurd bravery that comes with not knowing what works … when you don't know what works you will try anything. –*Joe Calloway*

Done is better than perfect. –*Sheryl Sandberg*

We cannot change what we are not aware of, and once we are aware, we cannot help but change. –*Sheryl Sandberg*

It's what you learn after you know it all that counts. –*John Wooden*

The biggest risk is not taking any risk … In a world that is changing really quickly, the only strategy that is guaranteed to fail is not taking risks. –*Mark Zuckerberg*

Move fast and break things. Unless you are breaking stuff, you are not moving fast enough. –*Mark Zuckerberg*

I think a simple rule of business is, if you do the things that are easier first, then you can actually make a lot of progress. –*Mark Zuckerberg*

Management is built on the totally erroneous assumption that there is one right way to learn and it is the same for everyone. –*Peter Drucker*

Whenever you see a successful business, someone once made a courageous decision. –*Peter Drucker*

Culture may be progressive for a certain length of time and then stop. When does it stop? When it ceases to possess individuality. –*John Stuart Mill*

Success is moving from failure to failure without loss of enthusiasm. –*Winston Churchill*

Success is not final, failure is not fatal: it is the courage to continue that counts. –*Winston Churchill*

A pessimist sees the difficulty in every opportunity; an optimist sees the opportunity in every difficulty. –*Winston Churchill*

You have enemies? Good. That means you've stood up for something, sometime in your life. –*Winston Churchill*

It is not enough that we do our best; sometimes we must do what is required. –*Winston Churchill*

A lady came up to me one day and said 'Sir! You are drunk', to which I replied 'I am drunk today madam, and tomorrow I shall be sober but you will still be ugly'. –*Winston Churchill*

To improve is to change; to be perfect is to change often. –*Winston Churchill*

All the great things are simple, and many can be expressed in a single word: freedom, justice, honour, duty, mercy, hope. –*Winston Churchill*

A lady once said to me 'If I were your wife I'd put poison in your tea!' to which I replied 'If I were your husband I'd drink it.' –*Winston Churchill*

Americans will always do the right thing; after exhausting all the alternatives. –*Winston Churchill*

New business concepts are always, always the product of lucky foresight. That's right – the essential insight doesn't come out of any disciplined planning process; it comes from some cocktail of happenstance, desire, curiosity, ambition and need. But at the end of the day, there has to be a degree of foresight – a sense of where new riches lie. So radical innovation is always one part fortuity and one part clearheaded vision. –*Gary Hamel*

Resilience is based on the ability to embrace the extremes – while not becoming an extremist. Most companies don't do paradox very well. –*Gary Hamel*

Dakota tribal wisdom says that when you're on a dead horse, the best strategy is to dismount. Of course, there are other strategies. You can change riders. You can get a committee to study the dead horse. You can benchmark how other companies ride dead horses. You can declare that it's cheaper to feed a dead horse. You can harness several dead horses together. But after you've tried all these things, you're still going to have to dismount. –*Gary Hamel*

Your boss is an older sibling. You'll always be respectful, but you won't hesitate to offer frank advice when you think it's warranted – and you'll never suck up. –*Gary Hamel*

In our company the trick is to change jobs in time to guarantee that the long-term pay-off you promised four years ago in your capital budget proposal becomes someone else's short-term performance target. –*Gary Hamel*

Instructions to the incoming manager, replacing a recently fired outgoing manager –

Here are three envelopes – when things get tough, open these one at a time.

After a few months things are tough, so envelope #1 is opened – it reads: "Blame your predecessor" … and it works like a charm.

Another few months pass and things are growing difficult again so envelope #2 is opened – it reads, "reorganise" … and again it works like magic.

Finally, about 12 months into the new job, things are getting really sticky so envelope #3 is opened – it reads … "prepare three envelopes".

–Anonymous

The only definition of a leader is someone who has followers. –Peter Drucker

Civilisations start to fail when they refuse to adapt. –Diamond

The pursuit of perfect accountability only creates suspicion – plants don't grow when we pull them up too often to check how their roots are going. –O'Neill

Hating, like a poisonous mineral, eats into the heart. –Hazlitt

Convictions are more dangerous enemies of truth than lies. –Friedrich Nietzsche

He who has a why can endure any how. –Friedrich Nietzsche

That which does not kill us makes us stronger. –Friedrich Nietzsche

Without great suffering there can be no great excellence. *–Friedrich Nietzsche*

And those who were seen dancing were thought to be insane by those who could not hear the music. *–Friedrich Nietzsche*

In heaven, all the interesting people are missing. *–Friedrich Nietzsche*

There are no facts, only interpretations. *–Friedrich Nietzsche*

To invent, you need good imagination and a pile of junk. *–Thomas Edison*

If you don't like change you are going to like irrelevance even less. *–General Eric Shinseki*

When all is said and done, more is usually said than done. If you will do today what others won't, you will do tomorrow what others can't. *–Keith J. Cunningham*

Never doubt that a small group of committed citizens can change the world. Indeed, it's the only thing that ever has. *–Margaret Mead*

Never doubt that a large committee (and various subcommittees) of interested stakeholders can suffocate even the greatest of ideas. Indeed, it's what incumbents do every day. *–Anonymous*

It is not the critic who counts; not the man who points out how the strong man stumbles, or where the doer of deeds could have done them better.

The credit belongs to the man who is actually in the arena, whose face is marred by dust and sweat and blood;

who strives valiantly;

who errs, who comes short again and again, because there is no effort without error and shortcoming;

but who does actually strive to do the deeds;

who knows great enthusiasms, the great devotions;

who spends himself in a worthy cause;

who at the best knows in the end the triumph of high achievement, and who at the worst, if he fails, at least fails while daring greatly, so that his place shall never be with those cold and timid souls who neither know victory nor defeat. *—Theodore Roosevelt*

Grammar: the difference between knowing your shit and knowing you're shit. *—Anonymous*

Imagination is more important than knowledge. *—Einstein*

The only antidote to poverty is wealth. *—Ron Baker*

The colossal misunderstanding of our time is the assumption that insight will work with people who are not motivated to change. If you want anyone to change, stay connected while changing yourself, rather than trying to fix them. *—Edwin H. Friedman*

The real task of leadership is to confront people with their freedom. *—Peter Bloc*

We want to create the business model that blows up our current business model, because if we don't, somebody else will. –LeBlanc

The German General Staff [the story goes] used to divide army officers into four categories: the clever and lazy, the clever and hard-working, the stupid and lazy and the stupid and hard-working.

The best Generals, the Germans found, came from the clever and lazy; the best staff officers emerged from the clever and hard-working; the stupid and lazy could be made useful as regimental officers; but the stupid and hard-working were a menace, to be disposed of as soon as possible.

True leaders don't create followers; they create more leaders. –J. Sakiya Sandifer

Ignore the spin that CEOs don't need to innovate – all the research shows –innovative companies are led by innovative leaders. –Hal B. Gregersen

Insanity: doing the same thing over and over again and expecting different results. –Albert Einstein

Politics is the art of looking for trouble, finding it everywhere, diagnosing it incorrectly and then applying the wrong potential remedies. –Groucho Marx.

The third rate mind is only happy when it is thinking with the majority.

The second rate mind is only happy when it is thinking with the minority.

The first rate mind is only happy when it is thinking. –A. A. Milne

Firms at the top of their S-curves of growth: the time when innovation dwindles and heavily bureaucratised companies seek minor new adaptations, packaging changes, and manufacturing efficiencies in order to wring the last gains of productivity from an essentially static industry that has already long passed its phase of fast history. –George Gilder

Auto companies at the very pinnacle of productivity had lost all room to manoeuvre. New developments almost never emerge from the leading companies in an industry. None of the carriage makers and buggy whip producers could create a saleable automobile, and the gaslight and candle businesses neglected the promise of electricity; slide rule people at Keuffel and Esser succumbed without response to the handheld calculator; just as IBM lagged behind other companies in adopting most major innovations in business machines, from copiers to word processors; and as even Texas Instruments finally became relatively rigid and uncreative in the microprocessor field. –Christensen

The very process of rationalisation and bureaucracy by which a company becomes the most productive in an industry tends to render it less flexible and inventive. –Christensen

Great minds discuss ideas; Average minds discuss events; Small minds discuss people. –Eleanor Roosevelt

First they ignore you, then they ridicule you, then they fight you, then you win. –Mahatma Gandhi

Persistence in the face of a sceptical authority figure is priceless, and yet we undermine it. Fitting in is a short-term strategy that gets you nowhere. Standing out is a long-term strategy that takes guts and produces results. If you care enough about your work to be willing to be criticised for it, then you have done a good day's work. –Seth Godin

Science progresses one funeral at a time. –*Max Planck*

Reasonable men adapt themselves to the world. Unreasonable men adapt the world to themselves. That is why all progress depends on unreasonable men. –*George Bernard Shaw*

Be regular and orderly in your life, so that you may be called an original in your work. –*Gustave Flaubert*

If someone from the 1950s suddenly appeared today, what would be the most difficult thing to explain to them about life today? I possess a device, in my pocket, that is capable of accessing the entirety of information known to man. I use it to look at pictures of cats and get in arguments with strangers. –*Anonymous*

What a piece of bread looks like depends on if you are hungry. –*Arabic*

A product is not quality because it is hard to make and costs a lot of money, as manufacturers typically believe. This is incompetence. –*Peter Drucker*

Do the best you can until you know better. Then when you know better, do better. –*Maya Angelou*

Man sacrifices his health in order to make money. Then he sacrifices money to recuperate his health. And then he is so anxious about the future that he does not live in the present or the future; he lives as if he is never going to die, and then dies having never really lived. –*Dalai Lama*

We are going to win, because we don't understand politics. We are going to win because we don't play their dirty games. We are going to win because we don't have a party political agenda. We are going to win because the tears that come from our eyes actually come from our hearts. We are going to win because we have dreams and we are willing to stand up for those dreams. We know all this as the power of the people is so much stronger than the people in power. –*Wael Ghonim*

Nothing is without risk. We are on a hunk of rock travelling at over 16,000 miles an hour around an exploding nuclear reactor. –*Ed Kless*

Pragmatism is not enough. Nor is that fashionable word consensus. To me consensus seems to be the process of abandoning all beliefs, principles, values and policies, so that what is achieved is something in which no one believes, and to which no one objects. –*Margaret Thatcher*

You know what the cloud is – it is simply the Internet.

Same thing.

So you are concerned about using the Internet?

Good luck with that. –*Anonymous*

A leader is one who sees more than others see, who sees farther than others see and who sees before others see. –*Leroy Eimes*

A leader takes people where they want to go. A great leader takes people where they don't necessarily want to go, but ought to be. –*Rosalynn Carter*

Our chief want is someone who will inspire us to be what we know we could be. –*Ralph Waldo Emerson*

Great leaders are almost always great simplifiers, who can cut through argument, debate and doubt to offer a solution everybody can understand. –*General Colin Powell*

The mediocre teacher tells. The good teacher explains. The superior teacher demonstrates. The great teacher inspires. –*William Arthur Ward*

If your actions inspire others to dream more, learn more, do more and become more, you are a leader. –*John Quincy Adams*

As we look ahead into the next century, leaders will be those who empower others. –*Bill Gates*

In the simplest terms, a leader is one who knows where he wants to go, and gets up and goes. –*John Erskine*

The leaders who offer blood, toil, tears and sweat always get more out of their followers than those who offer safety and a good time. When it comes to the pinch, human beings are heroic. –*George Orwell*

Always look for the fool in the deal. If you don't find one, it's you. –*Mark Cuban*

A leader is a dealer in hope. –*Napoleon Bonaparte*

Before you are a leader, success is all about growing yourself. When you become a leader, success is all about growing others. –*Jack Welch*

Leadership is a combination of strategy and character. If you must be without one, be without the strategy. –*US General H. Norman Schwarzkopf*

People ask the difference between a leader and a boss. The leader leads, and the boss drives. –*Theodore Roosevelt*

Leadership involves finding a parade and getting in front of it. –*John Naisbitt*

Leadership is the capacity to transform vision into reality. –*Warren G. Bennis*

To lead people, walk beside them. As for the best leaders, the people do not notice their existence … When the best leaders work is done, the people say, we did it ourselves! –*Lao-Tzu*

A good leader takes a little more than his share of the blame, a little less than his share of the credit. –*Arnold Glasow*

The final test of a leader is that he leaves behind him in other men the conviction and the will to carry on. –*Walter Lippmann*

The task of the leader is to get his people from where they are to where they have not been. –*Henry Kissinger*

No more romanticizing about how cool it is to be an entrepreneur. It's a struggle to save your company's life – and your own skin –every day of the week. –*Spencer Fry*

The task of leadership is not to put greatness into humanity, but to elicit it, for the greatness is already there. –*John Buchan*

Never tell people how to do things. Tell them what to do, and they will surprise you with their ingenuity. –*General George S. Patton*

The challenge of leadership is to be strong, but not rude; be kind, but not weak; be bold, but not bully; be thoughtful, but not lazy; be humble, but not timid; be proud, but not arrogant; have humour, but without folly. –Jim Rohn

Those who try to lead the people can only do so by following the mob. –Oscar Wilde

The led must not be compelled. They must be able to choose their own leader. –Albert Einstein

In periods where there is no leadership, society stands still. Progress occurs when courageous, skilful leaders seize the opportunity to change things for the better. –Harry Truman

Innovation distinguishes between a leader and a follower. –Steve Jobs

If you think you are leading and turn around to see no one following, then you are just taking a walk. –Benjamin Hooks

You cannot be a leader, and ask other people to follow you, unless you know how to follow, too. –Sam Rayburn

You do not lead by hitting people over the head. That's assault, not leadership. –Dwight D. Eisenhower

Strive not to be a success, but rather to be of value. –Albert Einstein

I attribute my success to this: I never gave or took any excuse. –Florence Nightingale

Nearly all men can stand adversity, but if you want to test a man's character, give him power. –Abraham Lincoln

Illegitimum non carborundum – Don't let the bastards grind you down. –US Army general "Vinegar" Joe Stillwell

Tend to the people, and they will tend to the business. –*John Maxwell*

Leaders think and talk about the solutions. Followers think and talk about the problems. –*Brian Tracy*

The fastest way to change yourself is to hang out with people who are already the way you want to be. –*Reid Hoffman*

The smartest thing I ever did was to hire my weakness. –*Sara Blakely*

You manage things; you lead people. –*Admiral Grace Murray Hopper*

Leadership is the art of giving people a platform for spreading ideas that work. –*Seth Godin*

Leadership is the capacity to translate vision into reality. –*Warren Bennis*

Leadership is the ability to hide your panic from others. –*Lao-Tzu*

Acquire worldly wisdom and adjust your behaviour accordingly. If your new behaviour gives you a little temporary unpopularity with your peer group … then to hell with them. –*Charlie Munger*

In my whole life, I have known no wise people (over a broad subject matter area) who didn't read all the time – none, zero. You'd be amazed at how much Warren reads –and at how much I read. My children laugh at me. They think I'm a book with a couple of legs sticking out. –*Charles T. Munger*

Fearlessness is like a muscle. I know from my own life that the more I exercise it the more natural it becomes to not let my fears run me. –*Arianna Huffington*

I think when you're buying jewellery for the woman you love, financial considerations probably shouldn't enter into it. –*Charles T. Munger*

Milo or Milon of Croton (late 6th century, B.C.) – A six-time Olympic victor in wrestling, and one of the most famous Greek athletes in antiquity, Milo kept on competing even well after what would have been considered a prime age for an Olympic athlete. –*Charles T. Munger*

Diligence is the mother of good luck. –*Benjamin Franklin*

Ancient sources report Milo would demonstrate his strength by holding his arms out, fingers outstretched, and no man could bend even his little finger. Another legend maintains he would train in off years by carrying a newborn calf on his back every day. By the time the Olympics arrived, he was carrying a four-year-old cow. –*Charles T. Munger*

Cicero, learned man that he was, believed in self-improvement so long as breath lasts and that the study of philosophy is an ideal activity, usually serviceable for old people all the way to the grave.

Give me a lever long enough and a fulcrum on which to place it, and I shall move the world. –*Archimedes*

Can anything be so senselessly absurd than that the nearer we are to journey's end, we should still lay in more provision for it. –*Cicero*

The fear of death is silly in that either you are going to a perpetual, better afterlife or you won't retain any pain if there is no such outcome. –*Cicero*

I've been quoted (out of context, of course) as saying my father is the second smartest person I've ever known, Charlie being the first. To keep peace in my family, I have no comment on such reports. —*Howard Buffett*

Simplicity is the end result of long, hard work, not the starting point. —*Frederick Maitland*

However, my particular approach seldom seems to get through, even to people of immense ability. Things usually die after going to the Too-Hard pile. —*Charles T. Munger*

You must know the big ideas and the big disciplines and use them routinely, all of them, not just a few. Most people are trained in one model, economics, for example – and try and solve all the problems in one way. You know the old saying: To the man with the hammer, the world looks like a nail. This is a dumb way of handling problems. —*Charles T. Munger*

You have to realise the truth of biologist Julian Huxley's idea that 'Life is just one damn relatedness after another', so you must have the models, and you must see the relatedness and the effects from the relatedness. —*Charles T. Munger*

When my friend Buffett and I left our respective graduate schools, we found huge predictable patterns of obvious extreme irrationality in the business world. This irrationality was grossly important in what we were trying to do, yet it had never been mentioned by our professors. Our solution, one we learned at a very early age in the nursery: Then I'll do it myself, said the Little Red Hen

So if your professors won't give you an appropriate multidisciplinary approach, if each wants to overuse his own models and underuse the important models in other disciplines, you can correct that folly yourself. –*Charles T. Munger*

Don't take too much advice. Most people who have a lot of advice to give – with a few exceptions – generalize whatever they did. Don't over-analyse everything. I myself have been guilty of over-thinking problems. Just build things and find out if they work. –*Ben Silbermann*

It is a good thing for an uneducated man to read books of quotations. –*Charles T. Munger*

Remember Louis Vincent's rule – Tell the truth, and you won't have to remember your lies.

I have always imagined that Paradise will be a kind of library. –*Jorge Luis Borges*

I have always disliked that reference of Charlie's about the raisins. But it does no good for me to say anything; he's going to keep using it anyway. –*Nancy Munger* –comment on Munger quote '*When you mix raisins and turds, you've still got turds*'.

Two roads diverged in a wood, and I took the one less travelled by, and that has made all the difference. –*Robert Frost*

Before you are a leader, success is about growing yourself. When you become a leader success is all about growing others. –*Welch*

What you measure is what you get –*what you reward is what you get. –Welch*

The consistent lesson I've learned over the years is that I have been in many cases too cautious. Almost everything should have been done faster. –*Welch*

You just have to pay attention to what people need and what has not been done. –*Russell Simmons*

Give a project visibility. Put great people on it and give them plenty of money. This continues to be the best formula for success. –*Welch*

Finding great people happens in all kinds of ways, and I've always believed, everyone you meet is another interview. –*Welch*

A cardinal rule of business: never allow anyone to get between you and your customers or suppliers. Those relationships take too long to develop and are too valuable to lose. –*Welch*

They pretend to pay us, and we pretend to work. –*Traditional Soviet Workers Lament*

The great lesson in microeconomics is to discriminate between when technology is going to help you and when it's going to kill you. –*Charles T. Munger*

There are lots of bad reasons to start a company. But there's only one good, legitimate reason, and I think you know what it is: it's to change the world. –*Phil Libin*

The iron rule of life is that only twenty percent of the people can be in the top fifth. –*Charles T. Munger*

The way to win is to work, work, work, work, and hope to have a few insights. –*Charles T. Munger*

You don't have to be brilliant, only a little bit wiser than the other guys, on average, for a long, long time. –*Charles T. Munger*

I have never let my schooling interfere with my education. –*Twain*

Nothing is too wonderful to be true. –*Faradays*

Work. Finish. Publish. – Faradays

If you want to change behaviours, you have to change motivations. –*Charles T. Munger*

An undertaker, of course, would look very unseemly if he were jumping up and down and playing his fiddle during the plague. –*Charles T. Munger*

I like the Navy system. If a captain ... turns his ship over to a competent first mate in tough conditions and he takes the ship aground ... the captain's naval career is over. –*Charles T. Munger*

Twenty years from now you will be more disappointed by the things that you didn't do than by the ones you did do, so throw off the bowlines, sail away from safe harbor, catch the trade winds in your sails. Explore, Dream, Discover. –*Mark Twain*

Are you a serial idea-starting person? The goal is to be an idea-shipping person. –*Seth Godin*

Well, if you're like me, it's kind of fun for it to be a little complicated. If you want it totally easy and laid out, maybe you should join some cult that claims to provide all the answers. –*Charles T. Munger*

Many of the legal doctrines are tied to other doctrines. They're joined at the hip. And, yet, they teach you those legal doctrines without pointing out how they're tied to the other important doctrines. That's insanity –*absolute insanity*. –*Charles T. Munger*

If you can't feed a team with two pizzas, it's too large. –*Jeff Bezos*

I'm always asked this question: Spoon-feed me what you know. And, of course, what they're often saying is, teach me now to get rich with soft white hands faster. And not only let me get rich faster, but teach me faster, too. –*Charles T. Munger*

The man who doesn't read good books has no advantage over the man who can't read them. –*Mark Twain*

The company that needs a new machine tool, and hasn't bought it, is already paying for it. –*Charles T. Munger*

Teachers open the door, but you must enter by yourself. –*Chinese proverb*

Those who say it cannot be done, should not interrupt those doing it. –*Chinese Proverb*

Balance is for tires and ballerinas. Work-life balance is a misleading expression. Life and work are not two different things, but intimately interrelated. The word "balance" is also untrustworthy; it's too obvious, not to mention a terminally boring idea. It conjures up the image of being stuck and immovable, yet in order to move forward you must unbalance yourself into a new set of possibilities. As my mentor George Gilder wrote: "Show me a success in any field, and I'll show you an obsessive. If your life is "balanced" by languid afternoons at the museum, you cannot develop a new business, break an important story, or make a contribution to the world … . Our task on earth — labouring in the service to others — can only be satisfied through hard and unbalanced work." –*Ron Baker*

Fools act on imagination without knowledge; pedants act on knowledge without imagination. –*Charles T. Munger*

There's no shortage of remarkable ideas, what's missing is the will to execute them. –*Seth Godin*

True courage is not the brutal force of vulgar heroes, but the firm resolve of virtue and reason. –*Charles T. Munger*

The silly question is the first intimation of some totally new development. –*Charles T. Munger*

Almost all new ideas have a certain aspect of foolishness when they are first produced. –*Alfred North Whitehead*

I read everything: annual reports, 10Ks, 10Qs, biographies, histories, five newspapers a day. On airplanes, I read the instructions on the backs of the seats. Reading is key. Reading has made me rich over time. –*Buffett*

There is an old two-part rule that often works wonders in business, science, and elsewhere: (1) Take a simple, basic idea and (2) take it very seriously. –*Charles T. Munger*

Everything should be made as simple as possible, but not simpler. –*Albert Einstein*

I had an early and extreme multidisciplinary cast of mind. I couldn't stand reaching for a small idea in my own discipline when there was a big idea right over the fence in somebody else's discipline. So I just grabbed in all directions for the big ideas that would really work. –*Charles T. Munger*

Far and away the best prize that life offers is the chance to work hard at work worth doing. –*Theodore Roosevelt*

You don't want your airplanes designed in too egalitarian a fashion. You don't want your Berkshire Hathaway's run that way either. You want to provide a lot of playing time for your best players. *—Charles T. Munger*

If you see a bandwagon, it's too late. *—James Goldsmith*

Psychological tendencies are important because they help explain how smart people are influenced to do illogical/irrational things. *—Charles T. Munger*

We are too soon old and too late smart. *—German saying*

If you would persuade, you must appeal to interest rather than intellect. *—Benjamin Franklin*

An ounce of prevention is worth a pound of cure. *—Benjamin Franklin*

Keep your eyes wide open before marriage and half shut thereafter. *—Franklin*

A small leak will sink a great ship. *—Franklin*

Especially fear professional advice when it is especially good for the advisor. *—Charles T. Munger*

You only have to do a very few things right in your life so long as you don't do too many things wrong. *—Buffett*

Granny's rule is the key — do unpleasant and necessary tasks before pleasant tasks. *—Charles T. Munger*

It is not greed that drives the world, but envy. *—Benjamin Franklin*

I feel that luck is preparation meeting opportunity. *—Oprah Winfrey*

You can always tell the man off tomorrow, if it is such a good idea. —*Tom Murphy*

Never underestimate the man who overestimates himself. —*Anonymous*

It is essential for a thinking man to assemble his skills into a checklist that he routinely uses. —*Charles T. Munger*

The principal job of those in control is to keep the people who don't matter from interfering with the work of the people who do matter. —*Charles T. Munger*

Section 4

Further Reading

Bibliography

No	Author	Books	Bibliography	Website	Twitter
PASSION					
1	Malcolm Gladwell	Blink	Gladwell, Malcolm. *Blink: The Power of Thinking Without Thinking. Revised Edition.* Little, Brown and Company, 2007	www.gladwell.com	Not available
		The Tipping Point	Gladwell, Malcolm *The Tipping Point: How Little Things Can Make a Big Difference.* Little, Brown and Company, 2006		
		Outliers	Gladwell, Malcolm. *Outliers.* Little, Brown and Company, 2008		
		David and Goliath	Gladwell, Malcolm. *David and Goliath.* Little, Brown and Company, 2013		
		What the Dog Saw	Gladwell, Malcolm. *What the Dog Saw.* Little, Brown and Company, 2009		
2	Simon Sinek	Start With Why	Sinek, Simon. *Start With Why: How Great Leaders Inspire Everyone to Take Action. Illustrated, reprint.* Portfolio/Penguin, 2011	www.startwithwhy.com	https://twitter.com/simonsinek
		Leaders eat Last	Sinek, Simon. *Leaders eat Last.* Portfolio/Penguin, 2013		
3	Mihaly Csikszentmihalyi	Flow	Csikszentmihalyi, Mihaly. *Flow.* HarperCollins, 2009	Not available	Not available

No	Author	Books	Bibliography	Website	Twitter
4	Gallup	First, Break all the Rules (Marcus Buckingham, Curt Coffman)	Buckingham, Marcus and Curt Coffman. *First, Break All The Rules: What The World Greatest Managers Do Differently.* Reprint. Simon & Schuster business books, Simon and Schuster, 1999.	www.strengthsfinder.com	https://twitter.com/StrengthsFinder
		How Full is your Bucket? (Tom Rath, Donald O. Clifton)	Rath, Tom and Donald O. Clifton. *How Full Is Your Bucket?: Positive Strategies for Work and Life.* Educator's Edition. Gallup Press, 2007		
		Now Discover your Strengths (Donald O. Clifton, Marcus Buckingham)	Clifton, Donald O. and Marcus Buckingham. *Now Discover your Strengths.* Simon and Schuster, 2001		
		Strengths Based Leadership (Tom Rath, Barry Conchie	Rath, Tom and Barry Conchie. *Strengths Based Leadership.* Gallup Press, 2009. Digitized 29 Aug 2011		
		Strengths Finder (Tom Rath)	Rath, Tom. *Strengths Finder.* Illustrated, reprint. Gallup Press, 2007		
		Go put your Strengths to Work (Marcus Buckingham)	Buckingham, Marcus. *Go put your Strengths to Work: 6 Powerful Steps to Achieve Outstanding Performance.* Illustrated. Simon and Schuster, 2007		
		Strengths Based Selling (Tony Rutigliano, Brian Brim)	Rutigliano, Tony and Brian Brim. *Strengths Based Selling.* Gallup Press, March 1, 2011.		
		Wellbeing (Tom Rath, James K. Harter)	Rath, Tom and James K. Harter. *Wellbeing: The Five Essential Elements.* Illustrated. Gallup Press, 2010		
		Decade of change (Geoffrey Brewer, Barb Sanford)	Brewer, Geoffrey and Barb Sanford. *Decade of Change.* Gallup Press, 2011		

No	Author	Books	Bibliography	Website	Twitter
		Power of two (Rodd Wagner, Gale Muller)	Wagner, Rodd and Gale Muller. *Power of two: How to Make the Most of Your Partnerships at Work and in Life*. Gallup Press, 2009.		
		Eat, Move, Sleep (Tom Rath)	Rath, Tom. *Eat, Move, Sleep*. Tom Rath, 2013		
PERSISTENCE					
5	Jim Collins	Good to Great	Collins, Jim. *Good to Great: Why Some Companies Make the Leap ... And Others Don't*. Illustrated. HarperCollins, 2001	www.jimcollins.com	Not available
		Built to Last	Collins, Jim and Jerry I. Porras. *Built to Last: Successful Habits of Visionary Companies*. Harper Business Essentials Series, HarperCollins, 2002		
		How the Mighty Fall	Collins, Jim. *How the Mighty Fall: And why Some Companies Never Give in*. Illustrated. Random House Business, 2009		
		Great by Choice	Collins, Jim and Morten T. Hansen. *Great by Choice: Uncertainty, Chaos, and Luck – Why Some Thrive Despite Them All*. HarperCollins, 2011		
6	Verne Harnish	Mastering the Rockefeller Habits	Harnish, Verne. *Mastering the Rockefeller Habits: What You Must Do to Increase the Value of Your Fast-Growth Firm*. Select Books Incorporated, 2002	https://www.gazelles.com/home.html	https://twitter.com/thegrowthguy
7	Napoleon Hill	Think and Grow Rich	Hill, Napoleon and Ross Cornwell. *Think and Grow Rich: The Original Version, Restored and Revised*. San Diego, CA: Aventine Press, 2004	www.naphill.org	https://twitter.com/NapoleanHill
8	Matt Ridley	The Rational Optimist	Ridley, Matt. *The Rational Optimist*. Reprint edition. HarperCollins, June 15, 2010	www.rationaloptimist.com	Not available
9	Martin Seligman	The Optimistic Child	Seligman, Martin, Karen Reivich, Lisa Jaycox and Jane Gillham. *The Optimistic Child*. Random House Australia, 1995	www.authentichappiness.sas.upenn.edu	Not available

No	Author	Books	Bibliography	Website	Twitter
		Learned Optimism	Seligman, Martin. *Learned Optimism*. Random House Australia, 2011		
		Authentic Happiness: Using the New Positive Psychology to Realize Your Potential for Lasting Fulfillment	Seligman, Martin. *Authentic Happiness: Using the New Positive Psychology to Realize Your Potential for Lasting Fulfillment*. Simon and Schuster, 2002		
10	Daniel Goleman	Destructive Emotions: A Scientific Dialogue with the Dalai Lama	Goleman, Daniel. *Destructive Emotions: A Scientific Dialogue with the Dalai Lama*. Bantam Books, 2004	www.danielgoleman.info	https://twitter.com/DanielGolemanEI
		Emotional Intelligence: Why It Can Matter More Than IQ	Goleman, Daniel. *Emotional Intelligence: Why It Can Matter More Than IQ*. Bantam Books, 1997		
		Primal Leadership: The Hidden Driver of Great Performance	Goleman, Daniel, Richard Boyatzis and Annie McKee. *Primal Leadership: The Hidden Driver of Great Performance*. Harvard Business School Press, 2001		
		The Brain and Emotional Intelligence: New Insights	Goleman, Daniel. *The Brain and Emotional Intelligence: New Insights*. More Than Sound, 2011		
PURPOSE					
11	Peter Senge	The Fifth Discipline	Senge, Peter. *The Fifth Discipline*. Currency, 1990. (Second edition, 2006)	Not available	https://twitter.com/petersenge
		Presence: Human Purpose and the Field of the Future	Senge, Peter, C. Otto Scharmer, Joseph Jaworski and Betty Sue Flower. *Presence: Human Purpose and the Field of the Future*. Crown Business, 2004		
		Presence: An Exploration of Profound Change in People, Organizations and Society	Senge, Peter, C. Otto Scharmer, Joseph Jaworski and Betty Sue Flower. *Presence: An Exploration of Profound Change in People, Organizations and Society*. Crown Business, 2005		

No	Author	Books	Bibliography	Website	Twitter
12	Daniel Gilbert	Stumbling on Happiness	Gilbert, Daniel. *Stumbling on Happiness*. Knopf, 2006	http://www.danielgilbert.com/	https://twitter.com/DanTGilbert
13	Adam Fraser	The Third Space: Using Life's Little Transitions to Find Balance and Happiness	Fraser, Adam. *The Third Space: Using Life's Little Transitions to Find Balance and Happiness*. Random House Australia, 2012	http://www.dradamfraser.com/	https://twitter.com/DrAdamFraser
14	Stephen Richards Covey	The Seven Habits of Highly Effective People	Covey, Stephen Richards. *The Seven Habits of Highly Effective People*. Free Press, 1989	https://www.stephencovey.com	https://twitter.com/StephenRCovey
		The 8th Habit: From Effectiveness to Greatness	Covey, Stephen Richards. *The 8th Habit: From Effectiveness to Greatness*. Free Press, 2004		
		Principle Centered Leadership	Covey, Stephen Richards. *Principle Centered Leadership*. Simon and Schuster, 1992		
		The Speed of Trust: The One Thing that Changes Everything	Covey, Stephen M Richards (son of Stephen Richards Covey). *The Speed of Trust: The One Thing that Changes Everything*. Free Press, 2006		
INCUBATE					
15	John P Kotter	Our iceberg is melting	Kotter, John P and Holger Rathgeber. *Our Iceberg Is Melting: Changing and Succeeding Under Any Conditions*. St. Martin's Press, 2006	www.kotterinternational.com/	https://twitter.com/KotterIntl
		Leading Change	Kotter, John P. *Leading Change*. Harvard Business Press, 1996		
		Buy-in: Saving Your Good Idea from Getting Shot Down	Kotter, John P and Lorne A. Whitehead. *Buy-in: Saving Your Good Idea from Getting Shot Down*. Harvard Business Press, 2010		
16	Chip and Dan Heath	Switch	Heath, Chip and Dan. *Switch: How to Change Things When Change Is Hard*. Random House of Canada Limited, 2010	http://heathbrothers.com	Not available

No	Author	Books	Bibliography	Website	Twitter
17	Inder Sidhu	Made to stick	Heath, Chip and Dan. *Made to Stick: Why Some Ideas Survive and Others Die.* Random House Publishing Group, 2007		
		Doing both	Sidhu, Inder. *Doing Both: Capturing Today's Profit and Driving Tomorrow's Growth.* FT Press, 2010	www.doingboth.com/inder-sidhu	https://twitter.com/indersidhu
18	Clayton M Christensen	The Innovator's Dilemma	Christensen, Clayton M. *The Innovator's Dilemma: When New Technologies Cause Great Firms to Fail.* Harvard Business Press, 1997	www.claytonchristensen.com/	https://twitter.com/claychristensen
		The Innovator's Solution	Christensen, Clayton M and Michael E. Raynor. *The Innovator's Solution: Creating and Sustaining Successful Growth.* Harvard Business Press, 2003		
		The Innovator's DNA	Dyer, Jeff, Hal B. Gregersen and Clayton M. Christensen. *The Innovator's DNA: Mastering the Five Skills of Disruptive Innovators.* Harvard Business Press, 2011		
		How Will You Measure Your Life?	Christensen, Clayton M, James Allworth and Karen Dillon. *How Will You Measure Your Life?* HarperCollins, 2012		
19	Scott Anthony	The Silver Lining	Anthony, Scott D. *The Silver Lining: An Innovation Playbook for Uncertain Times.* Harvard Business Press, 2009	http://blogs.hbr.org/scott-anthony/	https://twitter.com/ScottDAnthony
		The Little Black Book of Innovation	Anthony, Scott D. *The Little Black Book of Innovation: How it Works, How to Do It.* Harvard Business Press, 2012		
20	Maggie Osborne	Silver Lining	Osborne, Maggie. *Silver Lining.* Random House Publishing Group, 2000	Not available	Not available
21	Carmine Gallo	The Innovation Secrets of Steve Jobs	Gallo, Carmine. *The Innovation Secrets of Steve Jobs: Insanely Different Principles for Breakthrough Success.* McGraw Hill Professional, 2010	http://carminegallo.com/	https://twitter.com/carminegallo

No	Author	Books	Bibliography	Website	Twitter
		The Presentation Secrets Of Steve Jobs	Gallo, Carmine. *The Presentation Secrets of Steve Jobs*. McGraw-Hill, 2009		
22	Richard Brandt	The Click: Jeff Bezos and the Rise of Amazon.com	Brandt, Richard L. *One Click: Jeff Bezos and the Rise of Amazon.com*. Portfolio/Penguin, 2011	http://ideas.time.com/contributor/richard-l-brandt/	https://twitter.com/rlbrandt
23	Walter Isaacson	Steve Jobs: The Exclusive Biography	Isaacson, Walter. *Steve Jobs: The Exclusive Biography*. Simon and Schuster, 2011	Not available	https://twitter.com/WalterIsaacson
24	Steven Johnson	Where Good Ideas Come From	Johnson, Steven. *Where Good Ideas Come From*. Penguin Group US, 2010	http://www.stevenberlinjohnson.com/	https://twitter.com/stevenbjohnson
25	James Leighton	Alligator Blood	Leighton, James. *Alligator Blood: The Spectacular Rise and Fall of the High-rolling Whiz-kid Who Controlled Online Poker's Billions*. Simon and Schuster, 2013	Not available	https://twitter.com/JamesL1927
INSPIRE					
26	Gary Hamel	Competing for the Future	Hamel, Gary. *Competing for the Future*. Harvard Business Press, 1994	http://www.garyhamel.com/	https://twitter.com/profhamel
		Leading the Revolution	Hamel, Gary. *Leading the Revolution: How to Thrive in Turbulent Times by Making Innovation a Way of Life*. Harvard Business School Press, 2002		
		What Matters Now	Hamel, Gary. *What Matters Now: How to Win in a World of Relentless Change, Ferocious Competition and Unstoppable Innovation*. Wiley, 2012		
		The Future of Management	Hamel, Gary. *The Future of Management*. Harvard Business Press, 2007		
27	Liz Wiseman	Multipliers	Wiseman, Liz and Greg McKeown. *Multipliers: How the Best Leaders Make Everyone Smarter*. HarperCollins, 2010	http://thewisemangroup.com/about/our-team/	https://twitter.com/LizWiseman

No	Author	Books	Bibliography	Website	Twitter
28	Carolyn Barker	The 7 Heavenly Virtues of Leadership	Barker, Carolyn and Robyn Coy. *The 7 Heavenly Virtues of Leadership. Volume 4 of Management Today series.* McGraw-Hill, 2003		
29	Chris Lowney	Heroic Leadership	Lowney, Chris. *Heroic Leadership: Best Practices from a 450-Year-Old Company That Changed the World.* Loyola Press, 2003	www.chrislowney.com/	https://twitter.com/chrislowney
30	Stephen Baum	What Made jack welch JACK WELCH	Baum, Stephen H. and Dave Conti. *What Made jack welch JACK WELCH: How Ordinary People Become Extraordinary Leaders.* Random House LLC, 2007	http://www.stephenhbaumleadership.com/	Not available
31	Richard Branson	Business Stripped Bare	Branson, Richard. *BusinessStrippedBare: Adventures of a Global Entrepreneur.* Penguin Group US, 2011	http://www.virgin.com/author/richard-branson	https://twitter.com/@richardbranson
		Losing My Virginity	Branson, Richard. *Losing My Virginity.* Random House, 2011		
		Like A Virgin	Branson, Richard. *Like A Virgin: Secrets They Won't Teach You at Business School.* Random House, 2012		
		Screw Business As Usual	Branson, Richard. *Screw Business As Usual.* Penguin Group US, 2011		
INVEST					
32	Peter Drucker	The Practice of Management	Drucker, Peter. *The Practice of Management.* First Perennial Library, 1986	http://www.druckerinstitute.com/	
		The Effective Executive	Drucker, Peter. *The Effective Executive.* Harper & Row, 1967		
		The Best of Peter Ducker on Management	Drucker, Peter. *The Best of Peter Ducker on Management.* Harvard Business School Press, 2007		
		The Essential Drucker	Drucker, Peter. *The Essential Drucker.* HarperCollins, 2001		

No	Author	Books	Bibliography	Website	Twitter
33	Richard Watson	Future Minds	Watson, Richard. *Future Minds: How the Digital Age is Changing Our Minds, Why This Matters and What We Can Do About It.* Nicholas Brealey Publishing, 2010	Not available	https://twitter.com/richwatson
34	Peter Sheahan	Flip	Sheahan, Peter. *Flip: How Counter-Intuitive Thinking is Changing Everything.* HarperCollins, 2009	www.petersheahan.com/	https://twitter.com/PeterGSheahan
35	Howard Gardner	Five Minds for the Future	Gardner, Howard. *Five Minds for the Future. Leadership for the Common Good series.* Harvard Business Press, 2013	www.howardgardner.com	https://twitter.com/Howard_Gardner
36	Robin Sharma	The Monk Who Sold His Ferrari.	Sharma, Robin. *The Monk Who Sold His Ferrari.* HarperCollins, 1996	www.robinsharma.com	https://twitter.com/_robin_sharma
37	Timothy Ferriss	The 4-Hour Work Week	Ferriss, Timothy. *The 4-Hour Work Week. Expanded and Updated.* Crown Publishing Group, 2009	www.fourhourweek.com	https://twitter.com/tferriss
		The 4-Hour Body	Ferriss, Timothy. *The 4-Hour Body: An Uncommon Guide to Rapid Fat-Loss, Incredible Sex and Becoming Superhuman.* Crown Publishing Group, 2010		
		The 4-Hour Chef	Ferriss, Timothy. *The 4-Hour Chef: The Simple Path to Cooking Like a Pro, Learning Anything and Living the Good Life.* Houghton Mifflin Harcourt, 2012.		
38	David Wolfe	Superfoods: The Food and Medicine of the Future	Wolfe, David. *Superfoods: The Food and Medicine of the Future.* North Atlantic Books, 2009	www.davidwolfe.com	https://twitter.com/DavidWolfe
		Eating For Beauty	Wolfe, David. *Eating for Beauty.* North Atlantic Books, 2011		

No	Author	Books	Bibliography	Website	Twitter
		Naked Chocolate	Wolfe, David and Shazzie. *Naked Chocolate: The Astonishing Truth about the World's Greatest Food.* North Atlantic Books, 2005		
		Longevity Now	Wolfe, David. *Longevity Now: A Comprehensive Approach to Healthy Hormones, Detoxification, Super Immunity, Reversing Calcification, and Total Rejuvenation.* North Atlantic Books, 2013		
39	Victoria Boutenko	Green For Life	Boutenko, Victoria. *Green For Life.* North Atlantic Books, 2011	www.rawfamily.com	https://twitter.com/RawBoutenkos
40	Ricardo Riskalla	The Rawfit Diet	Riskalla, Ricardo. *The Rawfit Diet: Longevity, Beauty, Detox, Raw Food and Fitness.* Rawfit, 2013	www.rawfit.com.au	Not Available
LAW					
41	Steven Levitt and Stephen J. Dubner	Freakonomics	Levitt, Steven D. and Stephen J. Dubner. *Freakonomics: A Rogue Economist Explores the Hidden Side of Everything.* HarperCollins, 2011	www.stephenjdubner.com/bio.html	https://twitter.com/freakonomics
		Superfreakonomics	Levitt, Steven D. and Stephen J. Dubner. *Superfreakonomics: Global Cooling, Patriotic Prostitutes and Why Suicide Bombers Should Buy Life Insurance.* HarperCollins, 2011		
42	Nassim Nicholas Taleb	The Black Swan	Taleb, Nassim Nicholas. *The Black Swan: Second Edition: The Impact of the Highly Improbable Fragility.* Random House Publishing Group, 2010	http://www.fooledbyrandomness.com/	https://twitter.com/nntaleb
		Fooled by Randomness	Taleb, Nassim Nicholas. *Fooled by Randomness: The Hidden Role of Chance in Life and in the Markets.* Random House LLC, 2008		
		Antifragile	Taleb, Nassim Nicholas. *Antifragile: Things That Gain from Disorder.* Random House Publishing Group, 2012		
43	Daniel Kahneman	Thinking, Fast and Slow	Kahneman, Daniel. *Thinking, Fast and Slow.* Farrar, Straus and Giroux, 2011	Not available	https://twitter.com/DanielKahneman

No	Author	Books	Bibliography	Website	Twitter
44	Dan Ariely	Predictably Irrational	Ariely, Dan. *Predictably Irrational, Revised and Expanded Edition: The Hidden Forces That Shape Our Decisions*. HarperCollins, 2010	www.danariely.com/	https://twitter.com/danariely
		The Upside of Irrationality	Ariely, Dan. *The Upside of Irrationality: The Unexpected Benefits of Defying Logic at Work and at Home*. HarperCollins, 2010		
		The Honest Truth About Dishonesty	Ariely, Dan. *The Honest Truth About Dishonesty: How We Lie to Everyone – Especially Ourselves*. HarperCollins, 2012		
45	Charles T. Munger	Almanack	Munger, Charles T. *Poor Charlie's Almanack: The Wit and Wisdom of Charles T. Munger*. Donning Company Publishers, 2008	Not available	https://twitter.com/q_charliemunger
LEARNING					
46	Daniel Pink	A Whole New Mind	Pink, Daniel H. *A Whole New Mind: Why Right-Brainers Will Rule the Future*. Penguin, 2006	www.danpink.com	https://twitter.com/DanielPink
		Drive	Pink, Daniel H. *Drive: The Surprising Truth About What Motivates Us*. Canongate Books, 2010		
		To Sell is Human	Pink, Daniel H. *To Sell is Human: The Surprising Truth About Persuading, Convincing and Influencing Others*. Canongate Books, 2013		
47	Sheena Iyengar	The Art of Choosing	Iyengar, Sheena. *The Art of Choosing: The Decisions We Make Everyday – What They Say About Us and How We Can Improve Them*. Hachette UK, 2010	www.sheenaiyengar.com	https://twitter.com/Sheena_Iyengar
48	Jack Collis	Work Smarter Not Harder	Collis, Jack and Michael LeBoeuf. *Work Smarter Not Harder*. HarperCollins Publishers, 1995	Not available	https://twitter.com/jackcollis
49	Heidi Grant Halvorson	Nine things successful people do differently	Halvorson, Heidi Grant. *Nine Things Successful People Do Differently*. Harvard Business Press, 2013	www.heidigranthalvorson.com	https://twitter.com/hghalvorson

No	Author	Books	Bibliography	Website	Twitter
50	John Maxwell	Talent is Never Enough	Maxwell, John C. *Talent is Never Enough*. Pearson Education India, 2008	www.johnmaxwell.com	https://twitter.com/JohnCMaxwell
51	Ken Robinson	The Element	Robinson, Ken and Lou Aronica. *The Element: How Finding Your Passion Changes Everything*. Penguin UK, 2009	www.sirkenrobinson.com	https://twitter.com/SirKenRobinson
		Finding Your Element	Robinson, Ken. *Finding Your Element: How to Discover Your Talents and Passions and Transform Your Life*. Penguin UK, 2013		
52	Rory Sutherland	The Wiki Man	Sutherland, Rory. *The Wiki Man. It's Nice That &* Ogilvy Group UK, 2011		https://twitter.com/rorysutherland
53	David Maister	Strategy and the Fat Smoker	Maister, David. *Strategy and the Fat Smoker: Doing What's Obvious But Not Easy*. Spangle Press Media Group, 2008	www.davidmaister.com	
		Managing the Professional Service Firm	Maister, David. *Managing The Professional Service Firm*. Simon and Schuster, 2012		
		The Trusted Adviser	Maister, David. *The Trusted Advisor*. Simon and Schuster, 2012		
		Practice What You Preach	Maister, David. *Practice What You Preach: What Managers Must Do To Create A High-achievement Culture*. Simon and Schuster, 2012		
		True Professionalism	Maister, David. *True Professionalism: The Courage To Care About Your Clients & Career*. Simon and Schuster, 2012		
LEVERAGE					
54	W. Chan Kim and Renee Mauborgne	Blue Ocean Strategy	Kim, W. Chan and Renee Mauborgne. *Blue Ocean Strategy: How To Create Uncontested Market Space And Make The Competition Irrelevant*. Harvard Business Press, 2013	www.blueoceanstrategy.com	https://twitter.com/blueoceanstrtgy

No	Author	Books	Bibliography	Website	Twitter
55	Anderson, Chris	Free	Anderson, Chris. *Free: The Future of a Radical Price*. Random House, 2010	Not available	https://twitter.com/chrisa
		The Long Tail	Anderson, Chris. *The Long Tail: How Endless Choice is Creating Unlimited Demand*. Random House, 2010		
56	Tom Snyder and Kevin Kearns	Escaping the Price-Driven Sale	Snyder, Tom and Kevin Kearns. *Escaping The Price-Driven Sale*. Tata McGraw-Hill Education, 2008	Not available	Not available
57	Dr Reed Holden and Mark Burton	Pricing With Confidence	Holden, Reed and Mark Burton. *Pricing with Confidence: 10 Ways to Stop Leaving Money on the Table*. John Wiley & Sons, 2010	http://www.holdenadvisors.com/	https://twitter.com/reedholden
58	Thomas T Nagle, John Hogan and Joseph Zale	The Strategy and Tactics of Pricing	Nagle, Thomas T, John E. Hogan and Joseph Zale. *The Strategy and Tactics of Pricing: A Guide to Growing More Profitability*. Pearson Education Limited, 2011	Not available	Not available
59	Seth Godin	The Big Moo	Godin, Seth. *The Big Moo: Stop Trying to be Perfect and Start Being Remarkable*. Portfolio, 2005	www.sethgodin.typepad.com	https://twitter.com/ThisIsSethsBlog
		All Marketers Are Liars	Godin, Seth. *All Marketers Are Liars: The Underground Classic That Explains How Marketing Really Works – and Why Authenticity Is the Best Marketing of All*. Penguin, 2009		
		The Purple Cow	Godin, Seth. *The Purple Cow: Transform Your Business by Being Remarkable*. Penguin UK, 2005		
		Poke the Box	Godin, Seth. *Poke the Box: When Was the Last Time You Did Something for the First Time?* Domino Project/Do You Zoom, 2011		
		We Are All Weird	Godin, Seth. *We Are All Weird: The Myth of Mass and the End of Compliance*. Do You Zoom Incorporated, 2011		

No	Author	Books	Bibliography	Website	Twitter
60	Gary Vaynerchuk	The Thank You Economy	Vaynerchuk, Gary. *The Thank You Economy*. HarperCollins, 2011	www.garyvaynerchuk.com	https://twitter.com/garyvee
		Crush it!	Vaynerchuk, Gary. *Crush It!: Why NOW Is the Time to Cash In on Your Passion*. HarperCollins, 2009		
		Jab, Jab, Jab, Right Hook: How To Tell Your Story In A Noisy World	Vaynerchuk, Gary. *Jab, Jab, Jab, Right Hook: How to Tell Your Story in a Noisy Social World*. HarperCollins, 2013		
61	Jay Abraham	Getting Everything You Can Out Of All You've Got	Abraham, Jay. *Getting Everything You Can Out of All You've Got: 21 Ways You Can Out-Think, Out-Perform and Out-Earn the Competition*. St. Martin's Press, 2001	www.abraham.com	https://twitter.com/RealJayAbraham
62	Ronald J. Baker	Measure What Matters To Customers	Baker, Ronald J. *Measure What Matters to Customers: Using Key Predictive Indicators (KPIs)*. John Wiley & Sons, 2007	www.verasage.com/ronald-j-baker/	https://twitter.com/ronaldbaker
		The Firm of the Future	Dunn, Paul and Ronald J. Baker. *The Firm of the Future*. John Wiley & Sons, 2003		
		Mind Over Matter	Baker, Ronald J. *Mind Over Matter: Why Intellectual Capital is the Chief Source of Wealth*. John Wiley & Sons, 2007		
		Implementing Value Pricing	Baker, Ronald J. *Implementing Value Pricing: A Radical Business Model for Professional Firms*. John Wiley & Sons, 2007		
63	Edward De Bono and John C Lyons	Marketing without Money	Lyons, John C and Edward De Bono. *Marketing Without Money*. Pennon Publishing, 2004	www.edwdebono.com	Not available
64	Tim Williams	Positioning for Professionals	Williams, Tim. *Positioning for Professionals: How Professional Knowledge Firms Can Differentiate Their Way to Success*. John Wiley and Sons, 2010	www.ignitionconsulting.com	https://twitter.com/timwilliamsICG
65	Neil Rackham	Spin Selling	Rackham, Neil. *Spin-Selling*, Gower Publishing Company, 1995	www.neilrackham.com	https://twitter.com/NRackham

No	Author	Books	Bibliography	Website	Twitter
66	Charlene Li and Josh Bernoff	Groundswell	Li, Charlene and Josh Bernoff. *Groundswell*. Harvard Business Review Press, 2009	http://withoutbullshit.com/charleneli http://charleneli.com/	https://twitter.com/charleneli https://twitter.com/jbernoff
67	Edward Bernays	Propaganda	Bernays, Edward. *Propaganda*. Create Space Independent Publishing Platform, 2010		https://twitter.com/EdwardBernays1
68	Thomas Friedman	The World is Flat	Friedman, Thomas L. *The World Is Flat [Further Updated and Expanded; Release 3.0]: A Brief History of the Twenty-first Century*. Farrar. Strauss and Giroux, 2007	www.thomasfriedman.com	https://twitter.com/tomfriedman
69	Chris Brogan and Julien Smith	Trust Agents	Brogan, Chris and Julien Smith. *Trust Agents: Using the Web to Build Influence, Improve Reputation and Earn Trust*. John Wiley & Sons, 2009	www.chrisbrogan.com www.juliensmith.com	https://twitter.com/chrisbrogan https://twitter.com/julien
70	Zella Jackson	The Art of Selling Art	Jackson, Zella. *The Art of Selling Art*. Consultant Press, 1994	www.drzellajackson hannum.com	https://twitter.com/DrZellaJackson
71	Dale Carnegie	How to Win Friends and Influence People	Carnegie, Dale. *How to Win Friends and Influence People*. Simon and Schuster, 1936	www.dalecarnegie.com	https://twitter.com/DaleCarnegie
72	Dr Seuss	Oh, the Places You'll Go	Dr Seuss and Carter, David. *Oh, the Places You'll Go*. Random House, 1990	www.seussville.com	Not available

About the Author

Matthew Burgess is one of the founders of specialist firm View Legal.

Having the opportunity to help clients achieve their goals is what he is most passionate about.

As Matthew always works in conjunction with trusted advisers (whether it be accountants, financial advisers or other lawyers) and their clients, finding ways to fundamentally improve the value received by those advisers, and in turn their clients, has led him to develop numerous game changing models. Examples include providing guaranteed upfront fixed pricing, founding what is widely regarded as Australia's first virtual law firm, and more recently, developing a platform that gives advisers access to market leading advice and support for less than $1 a week.

Matthew's specialisation in tax, structuring, asset protection, estate and succession planning has seen him recognised by most leading industry associations including the Tax Institute, the Weekly Tax Bulletin, in the 2014 'Best Lawyers' list for trusts and estates and since 2015 in 'Doyles' for taxation.

Work is one aspect of his life Matthew loves, so there is no need to be constantly searching for 'balance'. His other great loves are:

- Family – they are profiled in various ways through the series of children's books he has written under the pseudonym 'Lily Burgess' – see **www.wordsfromdaddysmouth.com.au** and various TV commercials;

- Learning – going cold Turkey on television and most forms of media in late 2005 has radically increased Matthew's ability to study the great authors and inspired him to recently publish a book that explores the concept of 'true success' – see **www.thedreamenabler.com.au**

- Health – aside from being a foodie and swimming at least a 5km a week, Matthew installed a stand up workstation in 2007 and among a few other lifestyle choices, it changed his life.

Acknowledgement

This book is a result of contributions from countless people, each of whom I thank in a general sense. More particularly:

1   All of the clients I have been fortunate enough to assist over the years have had significant influence on me personally, and obviously, the stories of a number of them form the foundation of this book.

2   While I only know a handful of the authors listed in the bibliography personally, all of them also have had a significant influence on me, and again obviously, this book.

3   There have been countless people involved, as with any book production, in reviewing, editing, designing and ultimately publishing it. The contribution of each and every person is very gratefully acknowledged.

4   The team of people that I work with at View Legal have inspired me virtually every day for many years now. Personal thanks to Naomi Arnold, Patrick Ellwood and Tara Lucke.

5   Separately, thank you to former colleague Liam Polkinghorne, who devoted significant time and energy at a critical juncture in the drafting process to read the manuscript from cover to cover.

6   Finally, very deep and personal thanks to my family, and in particular, my immediate family. This book is the only tangible thing to show for them reading, researching, collating and writing. It also signifies the end, at least for the time being, of a project that in its current form has been around one year of focused effort and energy.

www.ingramcontent.com/pod-product-compliance
Lightning Source LLC
Chambersburg PA
CBHW061300220326
41599CB00028B/5718